BOMBER GROUP
AT WAR

R5689, N-Nan of No 50
Squadron, being flown for a Press
facility on 28 August 1942 by Sqn
Ldr Hugh Everitt DSO, DFC. On
19 September 1942, when
returning from a 'Gardening' trip,
Sgt E. J. Morley had both port
engines fail and crashed at
Thurlby, ending 'Nan's' career.
The Lanc was then 'immortalised'
as the subject of the pub-sign of
The Flying Lancaster in Desford,
Leics.
Courtesy OC No 50 Squadron RAF

BOMBER GROUP
AT WAR
Chaz Bowyer

LONDON

IAN ALLAN LTD

'There be of them, that have left a name behind them, that their praises might be reported. And some there be which have no memorial . . .'

Ecclesiasticus
Chapter 44, Verse 9

By the same Author:
Calshot, 1913-61
The Flying Elephants
Mosquito at War
Hurricane at War
Airmen of World War One
Sunderland at War
Hampden Special
Beaufighter at War
Path Finders at War
Albert Ball, VC
For Valour — The Air VCs
Sopwith Camel — King of Combat
History of the RAF
Guns in the Sky — The Air Gunners
Coastal Command at War
Spitfire
Fighter Command
Veteran Aircraft of World War Two

Edited:
Bomber Pilot, 1916-18
Fighter Pilot on the Western Front
Wings over the Somme
Fall of an Eagle — Udet

First published 1981
Reprinted 2000

ISBN 0 7110 1087 0

Published by Ian Allan Publishing

an imprint of Ian Allan Publishing Ltd, Terminal House, Station Approach, Shepperton, Surrey TW17 8AS.

Printed by Ian Allan Printing Ltd, Riverdene Business Park, Hersham, Surrey KT12 4RG.

Code: 0006/3

Addenda
Page 40: (Col 2 para 2) The aircraft in which Kirk was navigator was P4370 of No 144 Squadron.
Page 59: (bottom caption) The actual date was 17 July 1942, not the 1st.
Page 71: (bottom caption) The aircraft were No 49 Squadron Manchesters and No 83 Squadron Lancasters
Page 86: (caption) The Navigation Leader was Flt Lt E. Kilbey, DFM
Page 93: (caption) The NCO in charge was Flt Sgt Cyril Henshaw.
Page 115: (bottom caption should read) No 61 Squadron ground crews in front of Lancaster ME596 QR-H, at Skellingthorpe, 4 August 1944. The Lancaster was lost over Russelsheim on 12/13 August 1944.
Page 118: (top caption) The aircraft is a Manchester.

Contents

Introduction

Without question, No 5 Group was the most publicised Group within RAF Bomber Command both during World War 2 and, indeed, ever since. Even within bomber circles during the latter war years it became dubbed the 'Fifth Air Force' and 'Cocky's Private Airworks' — the last in deference to the high degree of autonomy granted to its most famous commander, Ralph Cochrane, by the AOC-in-C, Bomber Command, Arthur 'Butch' Harris. This 'glamour' image — at least, in the public eye — was enhanced by various outstanding exploits undertaken by some of its squadrons throughout the war, while in its ranks served some of the most colourful characters ever to fly in bombers. Former members of 5 Group almost invariably assert that 'their' Group *was* the best in Bomber Command; my correspondence files alone bear ample witness to such a perfectly understandable pride of community.

Yet beneath that imposed, if unsought facade of daring deeds and superlatives lay a much vaster effort by the host of un-publicised crews — air and ground — which contributed a lion's share to ultimate success. That 'silent majority' — as in every facet of RAF endeavours — forged the sword of eventual victory; its individual membership also paid the greatest numerical sacrifice. Thus this book is not intended simply as a regurgitation of the well-broadcast aspects of 5 Group, but is meant primarily as a necessarily limited yet utterly sincere tribute to that multitude of 'unknowns' — the 'ordinary' men and women who toiled, and too often died, carrying out a plain duty, with no thought of reward or craving for public acclaim.

It should also be unnecessary to emphasise that this volume is in no sense intended to assume the mantle of any academic history of 5 Group. Rather it is meant purely as an evocation of the period in which 5 Group achieved its greatest successes, and no less a reminder of a few of its 'failures'. Above all, it is offered as a small epitaph to those thousands of men and women of the Group who did not live to witness the final crowning of their doughty, selfless efforts.

In addition to the individual contributors in text, the following provided me most generously with the loan of documents, photographs, anecdotes, contacts, *et al.* To each I owe a debt of sincere gratitude: L. Bartlett DFM; C. Bowyer (*no relation*); S. Bridgman; J. Chatterton DFC; T. B. Cole DFC; L. Cottroll; C. Dack; E. J. Davis; B. Dowty; J. P. Flynn; D. Garton; R. Hammersley DFM; T. N. Hancock; W. Howarth; J. Lazenby DFC; H. Le Marchant; Sqn Ldr W. R. Lea DFC; Sqn Ldr H. J. Macdonald AE; S. H. Mansbridge DFC; G. McMahon DFM; Grp Capt F. L. Newall; L. W. Pilgrim DFC; F. Priestley; Sqn Ldr D. S. Richardson DFC; F. Slater; Sqn Ldr A. E. Smith AE; M. Stretton DFM; C. R. Street; J. A. Warwick; Flt Lt A. White RAF; A. E. Williams; W. H. Williams; Ogden, Dodd & Welch, Lincoln. And, as always, I have been privileged in my friends and their unselfish, ever-ready assistance; in particular here, Ted Hine of the Imperial War Museum; Sqn Ldr R. C. B. 'Chris' Ashworth; Sqn Ldr C. G. 'Jeff' Jefford; Bruce Robertson; Richard Leask Ward; E. A. 'Chris' Wren; Peter T. H. Green; Richard Riding; Alex Thorne DSO, DFC; Harry Pitcher DFM; 'Danny' Boon. And by no means least, Dave Gray of Walkers Studios, Scarborough who performed his usual 'magic' on fading and crumpled snapshots to produce superb prints for reproduction.

Chaz Bowyer
Norwich, 1980

Above: Official badge and motto of 5 Group, authorised by HM King George VI in March 1945. The lion motif was considered appropriately symbolic of the Group's qualities and courage. *MoD(Air)*

Background

No 5 Group, Bomber Command came into existence officially with effect from 1 September 1937 as one more facet of a rapidly expanding Royal Air Force. At that date it comprised a paring-off of units and personnel from No 3 Group, and temporarily was administered by a small staff at Mildenhall, while its original strength consisted of seven squadrons, thus:

Squadron	Aircraft	Based
44	Blenheim I	Waddington
50	Hind	Waddington
61	Audax & Anson	Hemswell
110	Hind	Waddington
113	Hind	Grantham
144	Audax & Blenheim I	Hemswell
211	Hind & Audax	Grantham

The first Air Officer Commanding (AOC) was Air Commodore W. B. Callaway AFC, whose appointment *per se* dated from 17 August 1937, and on 2 October he and his staff were able to occupy a large house, 'St Vincents', at Grantham and thereby create the Group's own headquarters. With the sole exception of No 44 Squadron, the whole group was flying obsolete, two-seat, biplane bombers, though plans were already in being for complete re-equipment with modern aircraft within the following 18 months or so.

Further 'muscle' for the new group came on 14 March 1938 when RAF Scampton and its resident squadrons, Nos 49 and 83, were transferred to the aegis of 5 Group; but within eight weeks three of the original complement were 'lost' when Nos 110, 113 and 211 Squadrons were despatched to the Middle East Command to strengthen the RAF presence there in the light of Italy's attack on Abyssinia. This reduction was part-compensated on 1 September 1938 when RAF Thornaby and its resident units, Nos 106 and 185 Squadrons, were transferred to Callaway's command. That same month also saw the issue to No 49 Squadron of a new, all-metal, monoplane bomber, Handley Page Hampden L4034, which arrived on the unit on 20 September 1938; the first example of the type to reach an RAF operational squadron. By November No 49 Squadron could boast a full complement of 12

Hampdens — the first all-Hampden unit in the RAF. Officialdom had already decreed that 5 Group would be wholly equipped with Hampdens, and the relevant dates of progression of re-equipment were:

Squadron	1st Hampden	Received	Fully equipped by
49	L4034	20 Sept 38	27 Oct 38
83	L4048	31 Oct 38	9 Jan 39
50	L4062	9 Dec 38	10 Feb 39
44	L4086	30 Jan 39	16 Feb 39
61	L4103	17 Feb 39	7 March 39
144	L4120	9 March 39	30 March 39
106	L4174	18 May 39	2 June 39
185	L4191	2 June 39	26 June 39

Below: St Vincents, Grantham, the HQ of 5 Group from 1937–43. The more modern extension to right was the operations block.
Ogden, Dodds & Welch

6

Left: Hawker Hinds of No 50
Squadron, 1937–38, including
K5749 (leading), K6741 (nearest)
and K6812.
Courtesy OC No 50 Squadron, RAF

Below: Hind K5401 of No 44
Squadron. This machine also saw
service with Nos 114, 15 and 611
Squadron before going to 27
ERFTS in 1940.

Left: Neat Vic formation of No 113 Squadron's Hinds shortly after arriving in Egypt, 1938.

Below: Bristol Blenheim I, L1304, which was initially allotted to No 110 Squadron on 1 September 1938, and left the unit a year later. *P. H. T. Green*

Bottom: Avro Anson, K6309, in No 61 Squadron's prewar markings. Later allotted to No 5 Air Observers' School, it crashed in the sea on 14 November 1942. *P. H. T. Green*

The initial establishment for 12 aircraft per squadron was raised with effect from 1 May 1939 to 16 aircraft, plus five 'reserves' on each squadron.

If the aircraft were new, the utilisation of them for their designed purpose was still very limited. Practice in pure flying, both singly and in formation, was pursued assiduously, yet apart from the annual war games — the last peacetime air exercises were held only two weeks prior to the outbreak of war with Germany — virtually no realistic warlike training was given to the young, eager bomber crews of the period. Indeed, at Scampton, for example, no Hampden crew had ever taken off with a full bomb load before war started. Moreover, none had any experience of landing by night under operational conditions, with or without a full bomb bay. The bulk of the bomber crews were junior officers, on short-term service engagements, with a thin vein of 'regular' airmen from such RAF backgrounds as Halton's Aircraft Apprentice School; while in most squadrons was a sprinkling of pilots and observers from various Empire countries who had come to England to join the RAF. All had passed through the very thorough peacetime training syllabi of the RAF — very few had ever heard a shot fired 'in anger'.

The aircraft in which they were destined to go to war, the Hampden, was already obsolescent in conception, with no physical potential for real improvement. A delightful aeroplane to fly, it lacked many essential features for modern air warfare; not least adequate defensive armament which, in 1939, consisted of three hand-wielded VGO machine guns at front and rear, plus a fixed

.303in gun firing forward for use by the pilot. Its narrow bomb bay could (theoretically) accommodate a maximum load of some 4,000lb, while the twin Bristol Pegasus radial engines gave a cruising speed of little more than 200mph at 15,000ft. The succinct summary of his private feelings of depression when taking up his appointment as AOC, 5 Group on 11 September 1939 has been recorded by Sir Arthur Harris in *Bomber Offensive* (Collins, 1947); 'For one thing the Group was equipped with an aeroplane which failed to meet many requirements of the normal specifications, especially with regard to comfort for the crew. It appeared to have little to recommend it except a very reliable type of engine and the fact that this particular aeroplane, the Hampden, had at least materialised in a hurry, and was available in some numbers; most of the other types were still largely on paper. The crews made the best of it and, being strong and reliable, the aircraft did a sterling job.' Some indication of Bomber Command's overall operational potential in that month is illustrated by the fact that Hampdens represented approximately one quarter of both its operational and reserve strength; and the doughty Hampden was destined to soldier on for nearly four years in operational use before being honourably retired to more mundane roles.

The Group's 'blooding' came on the first day of war, when nine Hampdens from Nos 49 and 83 Squadrons left Scampton for an 'armed reconnaissance' (sic) seeking the German Fleet, and nine more of No 44 Squadron from Waddington flew to the Schillig Roads on a similar mission. None found a target to bomb, many dumped their

bomb loads in the sea on the return legs, and all returned safely to base; among them two pilots, Guy Gibson and Roderick Learoyd, who were later to gain Victoria Crosses for 5 Group operations. Such daylight sorties, unescorted by fighters, quickly proved fatal, as on 29 September when 11 Hampdens of No 144 Squadron set out for the Heligoland Bight, and only six returned. Notwithstanding such casualties, the daylight sorties continued, though December 1939 saw the start of night flights on mining operations — 'Gardening' — which became a particular metier of 5 Group's Hampdens.

On the night of 24/25 February 1940 Hampdens of No 144 Squadron made their first 'Nickel' raid, dropping bundles of propaganda leaflets on Hamburg; the start of many other Group sorties dropping 'bumph' on enemy cities which, if totally unproductive in aim, at least gave the crews experience in night navigation and procedures. March 1940, however, saw a beginning of real bomb-dropping on Germany, partly by night but still including the hazardous daylight sorties; and as the result of particularly dangerous sorties in April two air gunners, Cpls A. D. Coldicott and J. Wallace, received the first DFMs to be given to 5 Group crew members. That month also saw the commencement of intensive 'Gardening' operations by the Group, and by the end of 1940 the Hampdens had flown a total of 1,209 such sorties, 'planting' 703 mines, and suffering the loss of just 21 aircraft. The first RAF attack on the German capital Berlin occurred on the night of 25/26 August 1940, and Hampdens from Nos 49, 50, 61, 83 and 144 Squadrons were part of the 81-strong force despatched. Of these, two failed to return,

Above: **The beginning of more modern equipment, exemplified here by Hampdens of No 50 Squadron at Waddington in early 1939. QX-D was L4076, initially delivered to the unit on 15 January 1939, and which saw further service with 14 OTU, then 415 Squadron RCAF before crashing in the sea on 6 September 1943.**
Courtesy OC No 50 Squadron

two others crashed on return, and a fifth was ditched in the North Sea.

As with the remainder of Bomber Command, 5 Group played a large part in the Battle of Britain by mounting a prolonged campaign of bombing German invasion barge build-ups in ports all along the Channel coast, and it was on one such sortie, 15 September, that No 83 Squadron Wop/AG, Sgt John Hannah, earned a Victoria Cross for quelling a mid-air fire in his Hampden and then assisting his pilot to navigate back to base. As the daylight battle over England finally petered out, operations were extended again against targets in Germany, and on 16/ 17 December Bomber Command instigated Operation 'Abigail' — the command's first 'area attack' — against Mannheim with 134 aircraft, 18 of which were Hampdens. Next day all Hampdens were officially relegated to night operations only, though in practice daylight sorties continued for many months to come.

On 1 November 1940, No 207 Squadron was reformed at Waddington for the purpose of introducing the twin-Vulture engined Avro Manchester to operations, and by February 1941 had commenced war sorties in the new bomber. Almost immediately the many technical problems inherent with operating Manchesters became apparent, and the following year brought a dispiriting saga of faults and failures, resulting in high casualties. By April 1941 a second

Manchester unit, No 97 Squadron, had begun operations with the type, and other squadrons converted to Manchesters during that year. The introduction of the design coincided with appalling conditions of snow, ice and sub-zero temperatures at the beginning of the year; though such conditions failed to deter 12 Hampdens from No 49 Squadron setting out for Germany on the night of 5/6 January — the *only* Bomber Command aircraft airborne that night. Nevertheless, such weather permitted only spasmodic operational effort for several months, and it was not until April that crews could concentrate on the latest priority objectives — the surface raiders *Scharnhorst* and *Gneisenau*, both lurking in Brest harbour and a constant threat to Allied trans-Atlantic convoys. Apart from such specific targets, the Hampden crews were used on a wide spectrum of sorties; an example being No 106 Squadron's activities in the period September 1940 to March 1941, during which the unit completed 1,230 individual sorties, dropped more than 800 tons of HE bombs, 'planted' 180 sea mines in enemy waters — and lost 55 crews which failed to return.

Additional strength for the Group came on 24 June 1941 when No 408 Squadron RCAF was officially formed and scheduled for equipment with Hampdens. After working up the unit flew its first sortie on 11/12 August — a raid on Rotterdam docks. The

Below: **By mid-1942 the Group had become an all-Lancaster formation, and thus commenced a truly heavy bombing offensive which was to continue until VE-Day, May 1945. Here a No 50 Squadron formation from Skellingthorpe, on 23 July 1943, is led by DV197 (VN-T) which was struck off unit charge a week later due to damage.**
British Official

same month saw a further unit added to the Group when No 455 Squadron RAAF was declared to be in existence at Swinderby from 6 June; though in the event it was not until late August that the Australian squadron was in a position to start operational flying albeit on a limited scale, and November before the unit was declared fully operational. On 19 December a third 'overseas' unit, No 420 Squadron RCAF, was formed at Waddington, and began its operational career on 21/22 January 1942 by bombing Emden with five aircraft, one of which was lost. Throughout the autumn and early winter of 1941 the Hampdens and Manchesters divided their main efforts between the continuing 'Gardening' campaign and direct assaults on Germany with particular attention to the large cities.

By early 1942, after a year of operating both Hampdens and Manchesters side by side, 5 Group's crews looked forward eagerly to the promise of bigger, better aircraft. On Christmas Eve, 1941, No 44 Squadron had received its first Avro Lancasters, and in early March had commenced Lancaster operations. By then a second unit, No 97 Squadron, had converted to Lancasters, and both units provided aircraft for a daring, low-level, endurance raid against a diesel engine factory at Augsburg on 17 April 1942, led by Sqn Ldr John Nettleton of No 44 Squadron who subsequently was awarded a Victoria Cross for his leadership on this occasion. The following month, on 30 May, Bomber Command made its first '1,000-bomber' raid of the war, against Cologne, and a 5 Group Manchester pilot, Flg Off Leslie Manser of No 50 Squadron, sacrificed his own life in order to save his faithful crew, and was awarded a posthumous VC. Re-equipment of other squadrons with the new Lancaster was relatively slow during 1942, and several squadrons were forced to soldier on in the ageing Hampdens and recalcitrant Manchesters until well into 1942. Indeed, it was a 5 Group unit, No 408 Squadron RCAF, which flew Bomber Command's ultimate Hampden sorties when Wilhelmshaven was raided on 14/15 September 1942; while the final Manchester sorties were those flown by 15 Manchesters participating in 'Butch' Harris's third '1,000-bomber' raid on 25/26 June, against Bremen's Focke-Wulf aircraft works. Thereafter Manchesters, with their near-identical fuselage and cockpit layout, became semi-ideal conversion trainers for crews of the units re-equipping with Lancasters.

During the same year 5 Group lost several of its veteran squadrons on transfer to other Groups or Commands. On 17 April — the day of the Augsburg raid — No 455 Squadron RAAF was given to Coastal Command, and was joined by No 144 Squadron in its future torpedo-bomber role with Coastal on 27 April. On 15 August a new bomber force was inaugurated within Bomber Command — the Path Finder Force (PFF), later to be designated No 8 (PFF) Group — and 5 Group's initial 'contribution' to this formation was No 83 Squadron, which moved en bloc to Wyton on that date. No 420 Squadron RCAF also left the Group, being transferred to 4 Group on 7 August. New 'arrivals' in replacement included No 57 Squadron which came from 3 Group on 4 September; and No 9 Squadron, another ex-3 Group unit, which moved to Waddington on 7 August and immediately started crew conversion from Wellingtons to Lancasters and was declared fully operational by 10 September; while on 7 November a new Australian squadron, No 467 RAAF, was formed at Scampton, moving to Bottesford later in the month to commence operations. To ease the overall conversion of 5 Group to an all-Lancaster force, 1654 Conversion Unit (CU) was formed 'internally', equipped initially with eight Lancasters, in May 1942.

The advent of the mighty Lancaster opened a new vista of bombing operations for 5 Group — and indeed the whole of Bomber Command. Its power, endurance, rugged reliability, relative ease of handling, and ever-increasing ability to lift heavier and heavier loads, endeared it to its crews, automatically providing a general uplift in morale. Portents of the Lancaster's future potential were three particular raids in October 1942. On the 17th a force of 93 Lancasters from 5 Group, without fighter escort, flew a dusk raid deep into enemy-occupied territory to bomb the Schneider Works at Le Creusot and nearby Montchanin; on the night of 22/23 October, 85 Lancasters, led by a PFF marking force, delivered a highly concentrated attack on Genoa without any losses; while on the 24th the first daylight attack on Italy was made by 74 Lancasters from 5 Group against Milan, using in many cases 4,000lb HC 'Cookies' and creating huge destruction on the ground. On 28/29 November two 8,000lb HC bombs were dropped on Turin by Guy Gibson and W. N. Whamond of No 106 Squadron — the first use of these giant blast bombs against an Italian target.

On 21 January 1943 the Casablanca Directive was issued defining Bomber Command's future offensive, and included the objective of '. . . undermining the morale of the German people to a point where their capacity for armed resistance is fatally weakened' — virtually a blank cheque for 'Butch' Harris's force to devastate any form of target, be it military or civilian. 5 Group at that moment comprised a total of 10 squadrons, with an operational strength of almost 200

Lancasters. On 28 February 1943 came yet another change in AOC when AVM the Hon Ralph Cochrane took over the reins of 5 Group; a position he was to hold for the next two years. Renowned for his restless energy and zeal, Cochrane, though long in Service knowledge and experience, had little *personal* experience of bomber operations of 1942-43 standards. However, he did have the complete confidence of the AOC-in-C, Bomber Command, Arthur Harris — in the words of Harris's deputy commander, Robert Saundby: 'Any attempts to convince the C-in-C that Cochrane could ever be wrong were inevitably doomed to failure'. This 100% support from Harris for Cochrane's ideas was to bear particular fruit for 5 Group a year later.

On 21 March another new unit came into being, No 617 Squadron, formed specifically to attack various dams feeding the Ruhr industrial complex, and on the night of 16/17 May, led by Wg Cdr Guy Gibson, 19 Lancasters were despatched from Scampton. The Möhne and Eder dams were successfully breached, but at a cost of eight aircraft and their crews. Gibson received a Victoria Cross for his superb leadership and personal courage; while No 617 Squadron was then earmarked for 'specialist operations only' in future — something of a volte-face from Harris whose explicit objections to any form of corps d'elite within his command had been forcibly expressed the year before when he had energetically opposed the formation of the PFF. Such precision attacks were also very much against Harris's preference for

Above: AVM Sir Ralph Cochrane KBE, CB, AFC who commanded 3 Group before taking up command of 5 Group. Born in February 1895, Cochrane originally joined the Royal Navy in 1912, served with the RNAS from 1915-19, then commenced a full career in the RAF. *IWM*

Left: HRH The Duke of Gloucester inspecting Lancaster R5868, 'S-Sugar' of No 467 Squadron RAAF at Waddington in June 1944. From left: AVM H. N. Wrigley RAAF, Grp Capt Bonham-Carter (Stn Cdr), HRH, and Wg Cdr W. Brill DSO, DFC (OC No 467 Squadron). 'Sugar' here displayed a bomb log of 107 ops, plus ribbons of a DSO and three DFCs, above an ironic quote from a speech by Hermann Göring, chief of the German Luftwaffe. *RAAF*

Above right: Probably the most-publicised exploit of 5 Group was the raid by Lancasters of No 617 Squadron against German dams on 16/17 May 1943, led by Wg Cdr Guy Gibson, who was awarded a Victoria Cross for this operation. Here, Gibson's crew is being debriefed in the early hours of 17 May at Scampton, watched by 'Butch' Harris and Ralph Cochrane. *IWM*

Right: 5 Group's ultimate operation was, somewhat appropriately, against Hitler's mountain retreat — the 'Eagle's Nest' — at Berchtesgaden, on 25 April 1945. Seen here is just part of the Lancaster stream heading over Walchen towards the target that day. *IWM*

general area attacks against large objectives; and directly opposed to his personal view that such forms of low-level heavy bomber tactics were '... almost without exception costly failures'. The bulk of 5 Group squadrons at this time were engaged in the 'Battle of the Ruhr' operations, and the Group was reinforced by the formation of No 619 Squadron on 18 April at Woodhall Spa.

The intensification of nightly operations over Germany throughout the summer of 1943 brought with it a parallel stepping-up of German defences; particularly in terms of night fighters, predicted flak barrages, radar detection devices, and other ploys. Against these the bomber crews introduced their own improving tactics and scientific aids, as on 24/25 July when the anti-radar foil strips known as 'Window' were first used in Operation 'Gomorrah' — four consecutive heavy raids which almost erased Hamburg from the map. Other weapons to be introduced at this time included the 12,000lb HC blast bomb, and on 15/16 September these were used for the first time in a distastrous raid by No 617 Squadron against the vital Dortmund-Ems canal. Five of the eight Lancasters despatched were lost before reaching the target, while a sixth failed to bomb. The following night another low-level attack by 12 Lancasters from Nos 617 and 619 Squadrons against the Antheor viaduct also failed to destroy the target, though on this occasion all but one aircraft returned to base safely. The problems of hitting a specific target with precision, even with specially modified aircraft by highly experienced

crews, were patently yet to be resolved by 5 Group.

The main force offensive continued apace as winter closed in, with the 'Battle of Berlin' commencing on 18/19 November; and in the same month two more units were added to Group strength when No 630 Squadron formed on 15 November, and No 463 Squadron RAAF came into existence from 25 November. At the same time Group Headquarters was moved to Swinderby and took up residence in Morton Hall. By the close of 1943 the Group could look back on a year of intensive operations, including several spectacular successes, but no little failure on other occasions. The continuing problems associated with accurate marking and bombing of any relatively small target had still to be resolved satisfactorily, despite the huge improvement in PFF techniques then in use. To Wg Cdr Leonard Cheshire, the latest commander of No 617 Squadron, the solution appeared to be one of emphasis on totally accurate *marking* of any target, and — in his personal view — this could only be achieved from low-level (as opposed to the contemporary PFF techniques at higher altitudes). Cheshire chose to use a DH Mosquito to test his 'theory' on the night of 5 April 1944 when an all-5 Group attack was made on a factory at Toulouse. On 24 April Cheshire repeated his success in a raid on Munich with results showing that 90% of the bombs dropped fell on target as a result of his low-level precise marking.

The most immediate result of Cheshire's marking successes was the transfer of three PFF squadrons to 5 Group, despite opposition from the PFF commander, Don Bennett, in order that Cochrane's men could henceforth provide their own marking aircraft and low-level techniques. Accordingly, Nos 83, 97 and 627 Squadrons were officially 'detached' to 5 Group in April 1944, and remained with the Group until the end of the war. The first five months of 1944 saw the whole of Bomber Command mount a particular offensive against enemy communications, rail systems et al — all part of the pre-invasion plans of the Allies — and after D-Day (6 June) such raids continued as back-up for the Allied land forces established in Normandy. On 8/9 June one such raid, against the important Saumur Tunnel, saw the first use of the 12,000lb DP (Deep Penetration) 'Tallboy' bomb; 19 of these being dropped by Lancasters of No 617 Squadron on the tunnel and completely destroying it. These were the first of a total of 854 Tallboy bombs to be dropped by Bomber Command before VE-Day. By September targets had included several rocket sites, rail centres, and waterways such as the notorious Dortmund-Ems Canal —

the latter being breached on 23/24 September by 5 Group aircraft — and the Kembs Dam on the Upper Rhine on 7 October by Tallboy-carrying Lancasters of No 617 Squadron. Other specific targets destroyed included the battleship *Tirpitz* in November 1944; again by Tallboy bombs, dropped by aircraft from Nos 9 and 617 Squadrons, led by Wg Cdr 'Willie' Tait. On the last day of December No 627 Squadron's Mosquitos rounded out the year by a daring attack on a Gestapo headquarters in Oslo.

The intensive pace of bombing was maintained throughout the early months of 1945, including another attack on the Dortmund-Ems Canal on New Year's Day, during the course of which Flt Sgt George Thompson, a wireless operator from No 9 Squadron, worthily earned a Victoria Cross for selfless sacrifice. On 14 March Sqn Ldr C. C. Calder of No 617 Squadron dropped the first 22,000lb DP 'Grand Slam' bomb which wrecked the Bielefeld Viaduct — the first of 40 more 'Grand Slam' bombs dropped during the final weeks of the war — all by No 617 Squadron aircraft. The ultimate war operation by 5 Group took place on the night of 25/26 April, and between then and 8 May (VE-Day) many Lancasters were employed in dropping food and supplies to occupied territories in Europe, and retrieving Allied prisoners-of-war from Europe and Italy. Almost immediately after Germany's surrender, preparations and training were put in hand for the eventual transfer of 5 Group to the Far East theatre of war against Japan, as part of 'Tiger Force', but the Japanese surrender in August nullified this move. AVM Cochrane handed over the reins of command on 15 January 1945 to AVM H. A. Constantine, who continued in command until the Group's ultimate disbandment on 15 December 1945.

The Group's war record had indeed been a prodigious saga of courage and sacrifice throughout the long years of war. Of the 32 Victoria Crosses awarded to any airmen during those years, nine had been awarded to 5 Group air crew members. Of the 47,268 men of Bomber Command killed or 'missing' throughout 1939-45, 11,990 had been men from 5 Group alone. Such men had been young in years — some never even reached the arbitrary 'majority' of 21 years age — yet all, with rare exception, had borne mature responsibilities far beyond their nominal years. Each had voluntarily placed his young life in jeopardy night after night in the pursuance of a clear duty. And if so many were not granted the satisfaction of witnessing the final victory over the oppressive cruelties of Nazi dictatorship, at least each had played his tiny yet vital part in that ultimate triumph.

Hinds & Hampdens

Squadron Leader Ken Cook DFC was one of the relatively small number of pilots who, having joined 5 Group in pre-1939 days, remained on operations with the same unit, No 83 Squadron, from its days of flying Hawker Hinds, through Hampdens, Manchesters, and finally Lancasters. His own recollections of the immediate prewar era on the squadron exemplify the general experience of most other pilots and crews in 1937-39 within Bomber Command:

'Early in January 1937 I finished training at 6 FTS, Netheravon and was posted on the 13th to No 83(B) Squadron at Turnhouse, near Edinburgh, with the rank of Sergeant Pilot. At that stage of my career I had a grand total of 156 hours and 20 minutes' flying time, in Tiger Moths, Hawker Harts and Audaxes. 83 Squadron, commanded then by Squadron Leader Dermot Boyle (later CAS), was equipped with the Hawker Hind, and although similar to the types I had previously flown, I was surprised and delighted to find that my first flight was to be solo to gain "experience new type" (as my log book confirms). Looking back now, I think that

was the real turning point between being told what to do (FTS) and being given full responsibility for an aircraft and crew. After half a day of solo flights — all of short duration — I "qualified" to carry a crew member (air gunner), then followed a succession of exercises, such as camera gun (front and rear), cross-country flights, high and low-level simulated bombing, formation practice, et al.

'In March 1937 the squadron proceeded to what was then called Practice Camp at Leuchars for four weeks, during which period we were able to drop real (practice) bombs on the bombing range and fire "live" ammunition from both front and rear guns. I don't remember the results being particularly spectacular but at least the exercises were more realistic than those simulated at Turnhouse, and at the end of the month we returned to base and resumed our normal routine.

'It is difficult to realise now just how few flying aids we had then. There was no Air Traffic Control, no runways, direction finding was in its infancy, and radio most

Below: Hind (believed to be K5528) of No 83 Squadron at Turnhouse, 1937, with full war load, ie four 112lb bombs under wings and crew's machine guns and ammunition.

unreliable; so map-reading and DR navigation were the order of the day. On one occasion I was detailed to carry out a formation practice with two other aircraft, with me as No 1 (Leader), and we were to practise close formation in line abreast, line astern, vic formation, etc. This was carried out at (roughly) 4-500ft for about 45 minutes, and it was then that I realised that we had full cover of cloud (strata-cumulus) below. It was early in the day and I assumed that it had formed over land and therefore should be clear over the sea, so I set an easterly course. After 15-20 minutes there was still cloud as far as the eye could see in every direction, so we returned on a westerly heading. Due to the lack of aids, previously mentioned, there was no help forthcoming from the ground, although we did have communication between the aircraft, and below that cloud was high ground. By this time I assumed, by dead reckoning, that we should be over the Firth of Forth and therefore safe to descend on an easterly heading. To play safe I put the formation on an easterly heading, instructed Nos 2 and 3 to remain on that heading and in level flight, while I descended through cloud. I was relieved to break cloud over the estuary and instructed the other aircraft to descend, and all was well. This little episode confirmed that, during that period of scant aids, it was essential to keep a mental picture of one's approximate position at all times.

'On 13 June a small number of aircraft were detailed to proceed from Turnhouse to Biggin Hill to take part in D/F exercises. We were despatched individually and map-reading was essential to try and remain as close as possible to the line previously drawn on the map. As the flight progressed the cloud base began to lower, until we were flying at tree-top level in deteriorating visibility. By then we had lost track of our position and decided to make a forced landing. Having found a suitable field we made a successful landing and, leaving the air gunner to guard the aircraft, I made my way to the nearest telephone to inform our flight commander of our predicament. Telling him we had force-landed near the village of Pocklington, in Yorkshire, his response was, "Oh no! Not another!" — apparently we weren't the only one to have force-landed en route to Biggin Hill. "Is the aircraft damaged?" . . . "No, sir" . . . "Do you think you can fly her out when the weather picks up?" . . . "Yes, sir" . . . "OK Sergeant, get your tail into the down-wind hedge and rev-up on your brakes before you let her go". Before leaving we learned we were within 10 minutes' flying time of Driffield and, after a successful take-off, landed there for refuelling.

'Though we had no Air Traffic Control as such, we were required to have a duty pilot on a rota system. He was ensconced in a wooden hut on the airfield and his duties included keeping his eye on the weather and wind direction, and adjusting the ground signals accordingly, and also the booking in

Below: Booted and spurred. Officers of Nos 49 and 83 Squadrons at Scampton in early 1937, in full Mess dress. Among many leading personalities here are Plt Off Guy Gibson (seated second from right), Sqn Ldr Dermot Boyle, OC 83 Squadron (behind Gibson), and Flg Off (later Air Cdre) Gordon-Finlayson (third from right standing).

and out of all visiting aircraft. A visiting pilot would normally book out for, say, destination Turnhouse with an ETA and that information would then be 'phoned to Turnhouse. On arrival the pilot would book in with the duty pilot and book out again before leaving. On one particular occasion a certain visiting pilot was booking out to Northolt and said to me, "Give me a minute or two to get height over the airfield, and when you see me set course pass *that* to Northolt as take-off time". Next day the press headlines were "Edinburgh to London at 400mph" . . !

'In mid-March 1938 the squadron moved to Scampton, near Lincoln; still a grass airfield but much larger with improved hangar and workshop accommodation. The surrounding countryside differed too, being so flat after the hills and mountains of Scotland. Our day to day routine did not change, but we now had access to bombing and gunnery ranges on the Lincolnshire coast offering something more realistic than simulated bombing. We were also able to carry out night landings on our own airfield; being equipped with night-flying facilities ie one Chance Light and X-number of paraffin flares. During the period at FTS we were given night-flying at odd intervals but, if memory serves me correctly, the curriculum did not include solo night-flying. I'd been with 83 Squadron almost a year when we were informed that we were to do some night-flying. Our grass aerodrome at Turnhouse was too small for such flying, so it

was arranged for us to proceed to Leuchars — for *one night* of night-flying! After 15 minutes' dual instruction by our CO, followed by 45 minutes of solo circuits and bumps, I became "qualified" to fly at night . . . My log book tells me that in our first six weeks at Scampton, I flew solo at night on three occasions. Two were of 30 minutes' duration, while a third was a local cross-country lasting 55 minutes.

'Most of June and July 1938 I spent on a navigation course at Shoreham, alternating between classroom and airborne in a DH Rapide — and if you ever fly in a Rapide, pray for smooth weather! On return to Scampton we learned we were to be re-equipped with Handley Page Hampdens. Having had little or no experience with twin-engined aircraft, coupled with the fact that due to its shape it was not possible to fit dual controls in a Hampden; we were allotted one or two Blenheim aircraft. I was given three hours dual instruction, followed by 20 minutes test for solo by Squadron Leader Cameron at Waddington — and away I went, "qualified" to fly a twin-engined bomber . . .

'On 31 October the squadron received its first Hampden (L4048) and during that period we carried out our normal routine on the Hind, with an occasional flight in a Blenheim to keep our hands in. Came my big day — 24 November 1938 — when I was to fly a Hampden for the first time. As no dual was possible, the only alternative was to

Below: **No 83 Squadron Hind 'bombing' demonstration for the public at the 1937 Empire Air Day, Turnhouse.**

Below: Hind K5443 in No 49 Squadron's prewar livery. Note Light Series and other bomb carriers attached under wings. This Hind later saw service with No 113 Squadron, before being struck-off RAF charge in 1941.

Above: **Hampden crews of No 83 Squadron at Scampton, February 1941. Ken Cook is third from left.**

Right: **Grp Capt Freddy Newall, a prewar pilot, who became B Flight commander on No 83 Squadron from June-September 1941, having already served with No 61 Squadron.**
Grp Capt F. L. Newall

Far right, top: **The office. Hampden pilot's cockpit. Note retracted pilot's seat in foreground — the only way in which an incapacitated pilot could be extracted from his seat in the air.**

Far right, bottom: **Briefing. Hampden crews of No 83 Squadron in the Ops Room — below SHQ — at Scampton, early 1941.**

crouch behind the pilot, who did a running commentary on his actions before and after take-off, in the circuit, and finally the landing. This instructional flight, conducted by our CO, Squadron Leader Leonard Snaith [Sqn Ldr L. S. Snaith AFC became OC No 83 Squadron from 11 July], lasted 20 minutes. Then he stepped out, I transferred to the pilot's seat, and off I went solo. Thinking back, it is difficult to believe that one could change from one type of aircraft to another with so few formalities. The next few weeks were spent familiarising ourselves with every aspect of our new aircraft; a mixture of cross-country exercises and circuits and landings.

'Apart from taking part in armament exercises at the end of January 1939, it wasn't until April-May before we really began to use the aircraft in the role for which it was designed. High and low-level bombing practice, as well as air-to-air (towed target) practice for the gunners, were carried out more frequently than in the past. During July we participated in the Regional Air Exercises on three days, and towards the end of the month we flew in formation from Scampton, via Tangmere, to Marseilles, and back to base — a total of eight hours' flying, and without doubt the longest flight we had ever undertaken. Up to this stage of 1939 I don't think many of us thought seriously about the possibility of taking part in a war. Certainly, that was what our training was all about, but surely there wouldn't be another war? We began to wonder as the war clouds gathered, and during August we took part in what were termed Home Defence Exercises, and even had one night — 27 August — allotted to night-flying. I had not flown a Hampden at night and, of course, dual instruction was not possible, so, just a couple of dusk landings and then into the dark for 30 minutes . . .

'On 1 September we were dispersed at very short notice to RAF Newton, near Nottingham, which was in the process of being built and therefore offered no facilities. Living quarters were only half-built but at least they had roofs on, and that was our accommodation for we knew not how long. As for eating, we each contributed to a "kitty" and visited local farms to buy what we could, mostly eggs and bacon. The next day, however, we were recalled to Scampton, but one of my engines refused to start and we were delayed. The fault was not rectified that day and on the following morning we learned that war had been declared. Eventually the aircraft became serviceable and just before leaving we heard rumbles and bangs emanating from the countryside to the east of Newton. We were convinced that we were hearing the result of enemy bombing — not until we were airborne did we recognise lightning to the east; a thunderstorm!

'Back at the base things were hotting up. During the previous night nine Hampdens had been armed with four 500lb GP bombs, and had been standing by since 0530hrs to operate against the German Fleet. At 1800hrs orders were received for six Hampdens — three from A Flight and three from B Flight — to "locate and destroy" the enemy Fleet in the North Sea. By 1811hrs all were airborne and by 2300hrs all had returned to Scampton, having been unable to locate their objective owing to darkness and bad weather. So ended our first day of war. What were our reactions? Difficult to be precise but — here we were, having been trained for this very objective and yet still not grasping the fact that it was really happening — and having little knowledge of what was to come.

'It was assumed that the squadron, having completed its first sortie, this routine would be repeated day after day for how long? We didn't know. We stood by at operational readiness for the next two days; then at 0815hrs on 6 September all bombs were removed and we were ordered to "scatter" to Ringway, near Manchester. No flying was carried out at Ringway and by 12 September we were detailed to return to Scampton to carry on with the normal training from dispersal positions on the aerodrome. During the period up to Christmas 1939 the squadron carried out only one further operational sortie, involving three aircraft, whose orders were to locate and destroy the German battleship *Deutschland,* believed to be off the Norwegian coast. Owing to weather conditions the ship was not located and the aircraft were instructed to return to the nearest aerodrome before dark. Two landed at Leuchars and one at Acklington after a flight lasting eight hours.

Above: Start up. A No 144 Squadron Hampden prepares to taxi out at dusk, Hemswell, 1941. Note wing leading edge Handley Page slots.

Right: Sqn Ldr Ken Cook DFC (third from left) and his crew of Manchester R5790, OL-F, No 83 Squadron, 1942. Having first served with No 207 Squadron, this aircraft later served with Nos 49 and 44 Squadrons and survived the war. The officer next to Cook was Flg Off J. L. Rowe, destined to die in Lancaster R5659 while bombing Essen on 8/9 June 1942.

'Notwithstanding the fact that those first few months were so inactive as far as operating against the enemy was concerned, there was always the daily thought lurking, "Is this it?". And then, when we were eventually stood down, a partial relief as thoughts turned to night life within the Mess or four miles distant in Lincoln. Though I can't speak for my contemporaries, I certainly thought that the odds on returning from my first sortie were not particularly good, and as for exposing one's self to the enemy at more regular intervals, the odds must surely diminish until . . ?

'Perhaps we didn't realise at the time just how unprepared we were. Imagine standing by for operations without ever previously having taken off with a full bomb load! Imagine the work involved in "laying" a paraffin flare-path on a grass airfield, only to find that the wind direction had changed and the whole layout had to be re-sighted accord-

ingly. Imagine the panic and time involved to extinguish all the paraffin flares when a single enemy intruder was in the vicinity. We did eventually design our own electrical flare-path at Scampton, utilising cable of appropriate length with electric light bulbs at intervals housed in petrol cans with the bottoms removed.

'To press the point of our unpreparedness a little further, my first operational sortie — April 1940 — was to drop a magnetic mine at a specified point in an estuary on the east coast of Denmark at night. Prior to this sortie my night-flying on Hampdens was five hours total, and the longest distance I'd flown at night was from Scampton to Oxford and return. I remember on returning from the Denmark sortie the feeling of sheer disbelief that we could really have flown so far, over so much water, and actually landed back at base . . . I can only contend that I had a guardian angel.'

Phoney War?

The period from September 1939 to 10 May 1940, on which date the German forces commenced their blitzkrieg ('lightning war') against the Low Countries and France, is constantly referred to by historians as the 'Phoney War' — the soubriquet invented by a sensation-seeking popular press. The title implies some seven months of virtual non-operational activity, yet nothing could be further from the truth. During that period RAF Bomber Command undertook a host of sorties against European targets, and suffered high casualties relative to the number of aircraft despatched. It was something of a 'testing time' for the RAF's bomber crews in particular. The myriad problems of undertaking operations in darkness, through weather conditions which, in peacetime, would have grounded all flying, and all the associated hazards, were obstacles which simply had to be overcome. Nor were these the only troubles met. Navigation in such unfamiliar conditions was more by 'Guess and God' than by an exact calculation; a 'defect' which was to bedevil the command in general for the first three years of the war.

Bomber crews of the RAF in late 1939 were given no specific number of sorties to accomplish before being considered for any 'rest' from operations ie there was no stipulated 'tour' of 30 sorties as was the case later. Thus crew members simply flew as and when ordered to do so, remaining on 'ops' until death, injury, or a wise unit medical officer decreed otherwise. Harry Moyle was an Air Observer with No 44 Squadron, based at Waddington, from the outbreak of war until August 1940. His account of just one particular sortie during those early days exemplifies the contemporary 'style' of bomber operations, and just a few of the hazards encountered:

'Thursday, 21 December 1939, dawned grey and cheerless as 96 young airmen, after hurried breakfasts and urgent briefing, clambered aboard their Hampden bombers, roared into the sky from Waddington and Scampton — 12 aircraft each from 44 Squadron and Scampton-based 49 Squadron — and circled Lincoln with recognition lights flashing as each took up his allotted

Left: **Sgt Harry Moyle leaning against a Hampden's tail at Tollerton, October 1939. He had yet to be officially awarded his brevet as a 'qualified' Observer.** *H. Moyle*

23

place in the main formation. Once having attained an orderly array, their leader eased them around until all were on course to the east. Their task for the day was to fly across the North Sea to the southern end of neutral Norway, then turn to search for 300 miles northwards along the coast in an attempt to locate the German battleship *Deutschland*, reported to be making a bid to "break out" into the north Atlantic. If found the *Deutschland* was " . . . to be destroyed", as our orders said rather optimistically. Four days earlier the battleship *Graf Spee*, damaged in a fight with three RN cruisers, had been scuttled in the river Plate on the orders of Hitler. It would indeed be a most acceptable Christmas "present" if we could now dispose of the *Deutschland*. (In fact, the *Deutschland* on this day was in harbour in Gdynia in the Baltic . . . !)

'Our Hampdens, now heading on a north-easterly course across the North Sea, each with its load of four 500lb GP bombs, were variously nick-named "Flying Suitcase", "Flying Frying Pan" or "Flying Tadpole" because of the narrowness of the fuselage in which the four crew members were contained, and the slender rear section which was in reality a boom supporting the tail with its twin fins and rudders. In spite of such epithets the Hampden was considered to be a good flying machine, particularly in regard to low-level manoeuvrability. Its qualities as a fighting machine had yet to be ascertained, but there was already an ominous question mark about the fate of five Hampdens from 144 Squadron which had disappeared without trace on 29 September 1939 during a sortie against German naval units in the Heligoland Bight. Rumours variously had it that they had been all shot down by anti-aircraft fire from destroyers, been blown up by their own bombs, or been destroyed by German fighters. (These five Hampdens, including the squadron commander Wg Cdr J. C. Cunningham, were in fact shot down by fighters from 1/ZG 26, I believe.)

'The two-hours' flight across the No Man's Land of the North Sea had a couple of highlights for me, as I sat hunched up in the rear gunner's position in the rearmost aircraft (L4089) of the whole formation. The first was when, after we had left our coast well behind, each of us tested our machine guns. It was always fascinating to see the tracer bullets curving away downwards to end in a splatter of splashes in the sea. By the time the four Vickers K guns and the pilot's single Browning had been fired, a smell of cordite pervaded the fuselage and seemed somehow reassuring. The second highlight concerned food. I had scrounged some bacon sandwiches to augment my flying rations and, feeling hungry and in a generous mood, decided to offer a share in these to the wireless operator, "Two-Tee". I hoisted myself on to the fuselage floor to sit between his feet and together we enjoyed our coffee break as we flew along at 180mph with the North Sea slipping away 1,200ft below us, with a layer of stratus cloud above us stretching monotonously to the horizon in all directions.

'Just before eleven o'clock, "Ferdie" Farrards, a sergeant pilot who was our navigator, called up the skipper, George Sansom, to ask him if he'd seen the two coasters up ahead of us. George said he had and that he was going to do a beat-up on one of them. He put our Hampden into a dive and when the coaster flashed into view from a few feet beneath us, I could see a couple of startled seamen looking up at us; from a mast at the vessel's stern a German flag stretched out in the wind, taut and taunting. The temptation to perforate this flag with a burst from my guns had to be suppressed as our orders forbade us to attack anything near neutral Norway's waters, unless it was the *Deutschland*, in which case it was to be a question of attacking first and answering questions afterwards.

'Our progression along the Norwegian coast for the next two hours was without incident; a few more coasters and fishing boats were sighted, as was the Norwegian coastline with its rocky promontories and fiords. Although the weather was gradually deteriorating, we did get one or two glimpses of snow on the higher ground, and using the expensive Leica camera entrusted to me I took a few photographs that should at least

prove that we'd been to Norway. By one o'clock we reached the end of our search area and, with mixed feelings of relief and anti-climax, turned to head for home, which was intended to be Lossiemouth in north Scotland. As we flew across the North Sea the weather became worse. The cloud base was so close to the waves that there seemed hardly room to fly in the space between, and heavy rain squalls then cut visibility down to such an extent that our two squadrons became separated and proceeded independently.

'After about an hour of really bad weather the cloud base lifted somewhat and we were able, for the first time during the trip, to climb to 3,000ft. Our general morale improved further when at about three o'clock George and "Ferdie", having noticed a change in the course we were steering, announced that they could see land a few miles to port, and that as we were steering a northerly, presumably Lossiemouth was up ahead somewhere. There now seemed little

point in me continuing my seven-hours' squat in the cramped rear gunner's position, and George agreed to my request that I be allowed to come up to stretch my legs. "Two-Tee" made way for me to crawl past his feet to pass through the doorway to the forward part of the fuselage, where I was able to sit on the wing spar behind the pilot in relative comfort.

'I lowered the armour plate extensions behind George's seat so that I could see what was happening, and opened the downwards-folding doors of the astro-hatch above my head so that I could enjoy the scenery. Ahead of us the rest of the squadron was spread out, making no attempt to maintain close formation. Our fuel supply would not last another hour and we had to find somewhere to land soon. It came as a great relief to hear George say that he knew where we were as he had recognised the coastline, and that in 20 minutes' time we'd be landing at Leuchars. This news was doubly welcome as most of us remembered Leuchars from our practice camp there just before war started.

We were not aware that the identification signals sent out over the North Sea by our squadron commander's aircraft had not been acknowledged, nor as our landfall was about 100 miles further south than had been intended that fighter squadrons were being sent up to establish our identity. Thus, knowing nothing of this confusion, when three Spitfires arrived on the scene and took up position behind us with the nearest only 20 yards from our tail, I waved cheerily from the astro-hatch and thought how nice it was that these fighter pilots had roused themselves from their afternoon slumbers to welcome us back to the motherland — what jolly decent chaps they were! After a minute or so the leading Spitfires dived away but the other two stayed on our tail and, in spite of friendly hand-waving, showed no sign of moving away. This was not at all the performance we expected. Our local fighter boys (No 504 Squadron at Digby) would have made half a dozen practice attacks by now, and this unexpected, inexplicable attention now became quite ominous. The uncertainty prompted me to ask George for the Very pistol so that I could fire the appropriate two colour cartridges of recognition, and as he removed the pistol from its stowage, all Hell broke loose.

'Our "friendly" fighters had opened up on us. I could hear the sound of their guns firing, the noise of the bullets hitting our aircraft was as though someone was emptying a tin of nails on a corrugated tin roof. My immediate reaction was to put as much aircraft as possible between me and those bullets. I dropped down beneath the pilot's seat to huddle against the wing root, and

Above: Vic-Three of No 49 Squadron's Hampdens, including AE354 ('S') leading, and AD980 ('V') nearest camera. The latter later became 'Y' of No 408 Squadron RCAF.

from this position could see vicious whisps of smoke as incendiary and tracer bullets whipped into the fuselage. Our first attacker blasted away with his eight machine guns and used up all 2,400 rounds in three long bursts, then dived away to make room for his companion to have a go. The fact that George had pulled back on the control column so that we climbed steeply made us a more difficult target for the second Spitfire, and after several short bursts he stalled and dived away. Our Hampden stalled and started to dive, turning as it went. I immediately scrambled back on to the wing spar to see what was happening. My first impression was that George had "bought it" because he was slumped over the control column. Realising that unless something was done pretty quickly we would dive straight into the sea, I leaned over him to pull back on the control column.

'It was a huge relief to see George now move. He gave a thumbs-up sign as he turned his blood-covered face towards me; fragments of his shattered windscreen had cut has face but he was not otherwise damaged and soon had the Hampden under control. Looking out from the astro-hatch I could see blue smoke streaming from both engines; our aircraft had suffered mortal injury and all George could do now was to crash-land on the sea. "Ferdie" emerged unscathed from the nose and just as I had decided to see how "Two-Tee" had fared, his face appeared framed in the window of the mid-fuselage door. I made signs that "Ferdie" and myself

were taking up our crash positions, and "Two-Tee" showed that he was OK as he too braced himself for the impact.

'As "Ferdie" and I sat back to back on the wing spar, hanging on to the fuselage sides, my main concern was that we wouldn't hit one of the lumps of rock that I'd seen sticking out through the waves. There was a juddering thump as we hit the sea. I released my hold, thinking we were down, but we bounced up again, and a few seconds later with an almighty splash we were down to stay. The second bump caught me unawares and I was thrown about a bit and ended up dazed in a heap on the fuselage floor by the wireless operator's door. Water was pouring in everywhere, and the dinghy pack was by my hand. It seemed a good idea to do something with it but I was unable to push it out of the astro-hatch because one of "Ferdie's" legs was in the way. "Ferdie" was standing with one foot outside the fuselage on the wing, and the other inside on the wing spar. I thumped his flying boot but before he could make a move the problem was solved — the Hampden sank.

'I finally shoved the dinghy out of the hatch and went to follow it, but the clips on the front of my parachute harness caught in the downward-folding door as the aircraft sank to the sea-bed some 80 feet below. The force of the water rushing through the aircraft effectively jammed me in the hatchway. I held my breath, felt pain in my eardrums, then with a crumpling crunch the Hampden L4089 reached its final resting place on the

sea-bed. I quickly freed myself and swam upwards to the surface, at first only visible as a dark green blur above me. I was hardly conscious that I had actually returned to the land of the living and would probably have not made any effort to stay alive had I not heard voices shouting. I looked about me and eventually saw George, "Ferdie" and "Two-Tee" clinging together in a huddle shouting to me "Blow your Mae West up!" There was none of the fancy CO2 nonsense with our Mae Wests; you had to blow them up in the old-fashioned way, which I did until consciousness faded away from me.

'The dinghy had not inflated and my three crew mates were a considerable distance from me, and when I came to my senses a few minutes later I was at the mercy of the waves. It was quite a pleasant sensation. Each wave as it picked me up gave me a short ride before leaving me to pass me on to the next one, and the larger waves crowned with white crests anointed me with cold spume. The possibility of survival seemed remote. It was the shortest day of the year, daylight was fading fast, and before long the cold water would penetrate my flying clothing; survival through the night must be nil. From my wave-top vantage points I'd seen no signs of life and my three comrades were nowhere to be seen. I was sure I was going to die. There was no feeling of fear, only sadness that my mother would be getting the dreaded telegram about me, and just before Christmas at that — or would they leave it until after? My past life didn't flash before me either — I don't think it ever does — and anyway, at the ripe old age of 18 I hadn't seen a lot of it.

'These melancholy meanderings were suddenly wiped out; a distant throbbing gradually increased in volume, until suddenly a couple of hundred yards away a fishing boat appeared, manned by (I discovered later) a father and three sons of the Pearson family from North Berwick. It stopped — was it picking up the other lads? — then started moving again. I shouted for all I was worth, waved my arms about, and the boat turned towards me. It was soon almost on top of me, a line was thrown, I grabbed it, was dragged to the side of the boat and hauled up on to the deck. There was one more anxious moment as one of the boat's crewmen moved towards me, knife in hand. He sensed my fear and reassured me that he only wanted to cut through my collar and tie which, if they shrank, would throttle me.

'It wasn't long before we were landed at North Berwick and our arrival caused quite a stir, particularly when it was realised we were "RAF boys", though I felt that even had we been Luftwaffe the kindly folk of North Berwick would not have been too hard on us. We were certainly the men of the moment, stars of the show, and I'm sure that had one been available a gilded coach with white horses would have taken us on our way. In the event we were bundled into what seemed like a laundry van and ended up in the kitchen of a nearby nursing home where we stripped off, draped in bath towels, plied with brandy, and settled in front of the cheery coal fire of an old-fashioned kitchen range until an RAF ambulance arrived to take us to Drem airfield, lair of our Spitfire assailants from No 602 Squadron. [Flg Off J. D. Urie, Plt Offs A. A. McKellar and P. C. Webb.]

'Ten aircraft from our squadron had landed at Drem. At the sick bay our Flight commander, Sqn Ldr Watts, assured us that the whole episode had been "... good experience" for us! Certainly, it didn't seem to have done any of our crew any harm; only George Sansom had superficial cuts about the face, but when I enquired of my fellow observer, Ken Lodge, how he'd acquired his bruised eyebrow, he told me that he had been hit by a bullet. (It was an incendiary and eventually caused the loss of the eye.) Their aircraft [L4090] had also been shot down by a No 602 Squadron Spitfire, and their wireless operator, LAC "Titch" Gordon, who tried to bale out, was killed in the attempt.

'From the sick quarters we were kitted out with brand-new, badly fitting uniforms from the clothing store. Then, without any badges of rank, we went to the Sergeants' Mess for some food. Our arrival through the blacked-out hallway into the Mess ante-room sent one Flight Sergeant disciplinarian into an apopleptic fit. He harangued us for appearing in the Mess with unclean buttons and took some convincing that we were not some of his raw recruits but genuine bomber squadron aircrew types whose visit to Drem was not entirely intended! We were taken into the kitchen where eggs and fried bread were frazzled for us. After eating our fill we were plonked down in armchairs and a variety of ground crew senior NCOs lashed us up with as much beer and whisky as we could consume. It was obvious that these tradesmen SNCOs were still not used to 18- and 19-year old aircrew Sergeants around a Sergeant's Mess, and I suppose it was high praise indeed to hear a Flight Sergeant with 1914-18 ribbons on his chest remark, "They're a chirpy lot, considering ..." Once back at the sick bay the combination effect of salt seawater, fried food and alcohol produced results that at least ensured that our stomachs left all traces of our experience behind us ...

'Next day arrangements were made for us to be taken back to Waddington, and we were tucked away in the luggage van of an LNER express which took us to Grantham, whence RAF transport whisked us back to base. An unexpected spell of Christmas leave came next, giving our crew at least a happy ending. In addition to the two aircraft lost from our squadron, 49 Squadron lost an aircraft which crashed on take-off from Acklington (where the squadron had landed), killing its four-man crew. So, of the 24 Hampdens which had set out on this sortie, two were at the bottom of the Firth of Forth, and another was a mangled wreck on land. Of the 96 crew members, five were dead and a sixth lost the sight of one eye — and none had fired a single shot, or dropped a bomb, in anger ... Perhaps our "unexpected Christmas leave" was part of the school of thought that it would be a good idea if we were "not available" to give evidence at the inevitable court of inquiry ...'

Ops in a Coffin

R.N.HAGGAR

'I joined No 106 Squadron in December 1940 after leaving my OTU at Upper Heyford. When I first heard that I was posted to 106, and that they were equipped with Handley Page Hampdens, my heart sank a bit. We had heard all kinds of stories about Hampdens and their abortive and costly daylight raids early in the war, and that they carried the dubious epithet of "The Flying Coffins" from their very narrow fuselage structure. In fact they did look, in their wartime drab green and brown camouflage, dark, very narrow and sinister — just like "flying coffins" indeed. I soon found out that the Hampden, in spite of its looks, was a stout performer. It flew delightfully on its two Bristol Pegasus engines, and the pilot's view well forward of the wing's leading edge was superb. The drawbacks were that they were certainly very cramped for space inside the aircraft, and if the pilot was hit or incapacitated the second pilot — who also carried out the duties of bomb aimer and navigator — as well as being reserve pilot — had to drag him out from his seat by pulling him backwards out of his position, and then crawl into the pilot's position; a feat which (unless the aircraft was fitted with "George") called for a combination of strength, dexterity, and a blind faith that the aircraft would stay on an even plane during which time this hazardous operation was accomplished. Defensive armament was not very good; twin air-cooled VGO's in the upper aft position, and similar in the lower aft position, and one fixed Browning firing forward and operated by the pilot.

'I'll always remember my first operational sortie. No 50 Squadron, up at Lindholme, were short of a 2nd Pilot/Navigator to make up a crew for a mine-laying trip to the mouth of the Gironde, down Bordeaux way. They gave 106 a ring at Finningley and I was told to get my flying kit and get up to Lindholme post-haste as briefing was that afternoon. A van soon ran me to the base and I met "my" crew and its skipper, Sgt Ormerod. The briefing and the raid was led by "Gus" Walker. We flew first down to St Eval to refuel and get mines aboard. I was pleased to meet an old buddy, Sgt Holley, who was flying Beaufighters with a squadron there (he was killed shortly after). After dark we took off over the Cornish cliffs, set course south across the Channel, Brittany and the Bay of Biscay, and down to the target area. We dropped right down to get a visual fix before commencing our dropping run, and successfully put one mine down in the correct channel. We then turned homeward and climbed to cruising height. It was a bright moonlight night and very cold, with good visibility. I calculated our ETA to make landfall over the Cornish coast, using the forecast winds which on the outward leg had

Below: **Hampden P1320, ZN-B of No 106 Squadron at Finningley, April 1940. Delivered to the unit on 4 January 1940, B-Baker crashed near Stamford on 25 November that year.**

proved accurate. Our ETA came and went with no sign of land or coast. We decided to persevere on the same course and after what seemed an age the coast loomed up and I tried to get a fix. Yet try as I might I couldn't get this coastline to fit my map. We cruised up and down for a while, then suddenly came across a lighthouse showing its light — not the usual wartime practice — and I finally identified it as Coningbeg — on the south coast of Ireland! The wind had altered direction and blown us westward, missing England completely and going straight over the Irish Sea. We soon worked out a new course to St Eval and duly arrived, being the last but one home.

'In January-February 1941 I was in the control tower at Finningley as Duty Pilot for the day — these were the days before Airfield Traffic Controllers. The weather was QBI (Quite Bloody Impossible . . .) and there was a complete clamp on flying with a low cloud-base, drizzling rain and very poor visibility. I was looking out of the tower window when suddenly, nipping smartly below cloud, a German Heinkel came hurtling across the airfield, dropping its bomb load as a "stick". The bomb line came directly towards the tower, the last bomb coming down right

behind the tower through a hangar roof. Fortunately it was a dud and those which exploded on the airfield had not done any real damage. Five minutes *after* the intruder had disappeared into the low cloud, the telephone rang. It was from Group. "RED ALERT! IMMEDIATE!!" — they said. My reply was unprintable . . .

'In early Spring 1941, No 106 Squadron received orders to move to Coningsby, a new airfield some 12 miles north of Boston in Lincolnshire. Everything was new and many buildings in only partial state of completion. Mains and sewers were still being laid, but (if

Above: Hampden Z-Zebra, No 50 Squadron, Swinderby, being prepared for a sortie.
Courtesy OC No 50 Squadron RAF

30

memory's correct) the officers' and sergeants' Messes were more or less completed. The equipment and most personnel went down from Finningley by road, but I took several ground crew as passengers when we flew to Coningsby as they seldom had an opportunity for a flight. The whole landscape was snow-covered and I had to circle Coningsby several times before I was sure I had the correct airfield. There was no runway and the whole time I remained at Coningsby it remained a grass-covered base. "A" and "B" Flight offices were in a long, low hut to the west of the main hangar on the perimeter track and rough, broken ground lay between these and the Sergeants' Mess. No 106 was dispersed mainly on the west and south side of the airfield, while the east side was kept for eventual occupation by No 97 Squadron.

'We soon "opened shop" and during that Spring one of our favourite targets were our old friends *Scharnhorst* and *Gneisenau* at Brest, and many a raid was directed at these two vessels. They were difficult targets, small (from 15,000 feet), well camouflaged, with very strong flak defences. It was on one of these raids that we lost Wg Cdr P. J. Polglase, our CO. Other French towns on our target list included La Pallice and Lorient.

These raids were part of the general pattern of the Battle of the Atlantic then being fought. Over Germany itself the main effort was against places which were to be devastated later in the war — Cologne, Hamburg, Bremen, Wuppertal, Essen, Dusseldorf, Hamm and the Rhur.

'My first few trips were as 2nd pilot-cum-nav-cum-bomb aimer to Flt Lt Altman, but in due time I was sent to do a captain's course at Cottesmore, then returned to Coningsby to form my own crew, and was allotted my own aircraft "X — X-Ray". My second pilot was Sgt Freddie Fry, while the W/Ops and AGs were Sgts Charlton, Earnsley, Bingley and, sometimes, Flt Sgts Hammett or McKenzie. We were a happy crowd and suffered no casualties until early one morning after our 18th trip together. Poor old Bingley, who was riding on the running board of the dispersal truck on the way to HQ for de-briefing, slipped off (muddy flying boots from the dispersal area) and went under the rear wheel of the vehicle. He was badly hurt and died next day in hospital. Hammett and McKenzie were prewar regulars, and proudly displayed their "Flying Bullet" brass AG's insignia on the right arm of their uniform jackets.

31

Above: Honour the brave. HM King George VI presenting a DFM to Cpl John 'Jock' Wallace, from Barrhead, Renfrewshire, at Lindholme, early 1940. Wallace, a W/Op/AG with No 50 Squadron, 'earned' his award during an attack on Christiansand, Norway, and was one of the first pair of DFM awards within 5 Group.
Courtesy OC No 50 Squadron RAF

Far right, top: Sgt A. W. Wood looks down from the bomb-aiming position of his Hampden, No 408 Squadron RCAF, at Syerston, 30 September 1941.
Public Archives of Canada

Far right, bottom: The Wireless Operator/Air Gunner's cupola in a Hampden. Twin Vickers Gas-operated (VGO) machine guns, with a Mk 1 Reflector Sight, are supplemented by a locally-made form of gun travel interrupter, riveted to fuselage top, to prevent AGs shooting at their own tail unit.

'It was about this time that some bright spark dreamed up the idea of "Razzle". This was the code word for small "sandwiches" of leather inside which was placed a small amount of phosphorous. These were stored in tins of alcohol and when taken out and dried, burst into flames. The bright idea was to scatter these over the (hopefully) dry parts of German forests and crop lands and create large fires to help the war effort. In order to push these out of the aircraft Hampdens were fitted with a metal chute in the bomb-aiming position — it looked like a chopped-off elephant's trunk. Complete with alcohol-filled tins of "Razzle" we set off to spread gloom and terror in Germany by starting "uncontrollable" fires — in practice it didn't quite work out that way. Nobody had paused to consider the airflow around a Hampden in flight, and the more desperately we tried to ram "Razzles" down the chute, the more they'd be violently blown back into the aircraft by the slipstream. The net result was that everybody ended up with their machines full of the damn things — which, on drying out, would commence to burn! Needless to say many a crew made a somewhat red-faced return to base, where for days afterwards our ground crews were still looking in odd corners for any errant "Razzles". The experiment was NOT repeated . . .

'About July 1941 it was suggested that a night operation flying *in formation* might be possible, and a combined load dropping all together might be more effective than operating singly. Accordingly, three Hampdens were detailed to attempt this, and I was picked to participate. The target, as far as I recollect, was an obscure factory deep in south Germany, in the general area of Augsburg. A bright full moon night was selected, our aircraft were fitted on the outside of the trailing edges with a dim blue light to assist station-keeping — something like a glim lamp — and we duly took off; with myself as right-hand man of the formation. Initially everything went very well, flying in a loose Vic formation was no trouble in the bright moonlight, and at times we flew quite close together. We stayed that way nearly all the way to the target, but when in the near vicinity my navigator pointed out that the leader was taking us away from the target area — he seemed to be unsure of his position. I broke formation and the other two disappeared into the night. We made a re-run, bombed the target as well as we could, then made track for home. Both the other Hampdens returned safely, but they too had split formation just after I had for the same reason. Which of us bombed the correct target was never established — though, naturally, I like to believe it was us — but we at least proved that on a bright night, with a full moon, flying in formation was perfectly feasible.

At this period, before the Japanese had come into the war and Holland was Nazi-occupied, we used to drop morale-lifting tea-bags over the country when on normal sorties. The tea, which came from the Dutch East Indies (now Indonesia) were the same size as present-day tea-bags but had a small Dutch flag attached and a message in Dutch on the other side. We dropped thousands of them but due to the shortage of tea at home some of our chaps often grabbed a few to take home on leaves.

'As I have said, in my time Coningsby was an all-grass field. For night flying a flare path had to be laid into wind in the form of an inverted L or T. In the beginning we used goose-neck flares, but later used a long cable with low-wattage lights, shielded from direct view above, at intervals along the cable, or a series of small, battery-operated lights called glim lamps. Responsibility for laying and operating the flare path was that of the duty pilot ("Paraffin Pete" in contemporary slang) for any particular night. At the landing end of the flare path was a Chance Light — a large neon red-coloured light flashing the airfield's identification code letters. This light was mobile and driven by a diesel generator. After the first aircraft had taken off the remainder of the squadron took off independently and the flare path was then doused until further required. When the flare path was illuminated we had to keep a sharp eye on the control tower, because if there was a Red Alert we had to run like Hell and put all lights off until we received an all-clear. These instructions were given to us by a red or green Aldis Lamp. One particularly bad night when I was duty pilot the weather closed right in with swirling fog just before the first of the squadron was due back. Normal flares were useless in such poor visibility, so we used the emergency Money Flares — similar to round drums of paraffin with large "wick" swabs being continually soaked in the liquid. They burned with a flame about three or four feet high and we had to keep driving up and down the flare path keeping the flares replenished and alight. In such fog, gloom and smoke, landing was a nightmare, and aircraft were coming in as best they could; some landing up the flare path, some down it, and some both sides together — yet all landed safely.

'Of the "mechanics" of flying a bombing sortie over Germany in 1941, I chiefly remember the following facets. Approaching the enemy coast and all the way to the target, I used to carry out a gentle weaving pattern of flying the course; first about ten degrees to port and then slowly back on course, then ten degrees to starboard and so on. The idea —

passed on to me by my first skipper — was to make it more difficult for any stalking night fighter to line us up for treatment. Over the target, of course, it was straight and level for the final run-in. Another trick we used to practise was to de-synchronise our motors every so often in the fond hope that this would fox any sound locators. The notion was probably totally erroneous but at the time we thought it helped. As one would expect, our chief troubles were flak and weather; night fighters (in my time) were not quite so lethal as they became subsequently. This was well before the idea of any "main bomber stream"; we all operated independently and therefore, presumably, offered more scattered targets.

'As for the weather, apart from the always unpleasant possibility of bad visibility back at base, my personal dislike was ice accretion. Several times when flying through cumulo-nimbus over the sea, outward-bound and climbing, we had to go through those black, towering mountains of cloud. Static electricity used to run all round the windscreen windows, and in icing conditions chunks of solid ice were flung off the prop blades and rattled against the fuselage. Deep inside these clouds it was jet black, with only the dim light of the instruments. The severe turbulence tossed the aircraft around and I had to use all controls to try to keep her steady, while sparks of static danced all around. If there was a particular very high one ahead on our track I always tried, if possible, to go round instead of through — some tops reached well above 20,000 feet, which was just a bit too high for a war-loaded Hampden.

'Aerial navigation at that period of the war was practically all DR — "Deduced" or "Dead" Reckoning — and map reading at night, which meant that there had to be a full moon to operate. We had no GEE, H2S or OBOE then. I believe that if in trouble we could have received a DF radio fix by trans-mitting and having our position plotted by cross-bearings and passed on to our radio operator, but this would have meant very serious breaking of the radio-silence orders, so I (at least) never had to use it. The tools of our trade were Mercator Charts for the plot, plus topographical and target maps, aided by a Dalton Computor, parallel rules, and a pair of dividers. We had to rely almost entirely on the forecast winds at various heights. Navigation was done by the second pilot, whilst astro-navigation was very difficult in a Hampden. Lacking a proper astro-dome in a Hampden meant opening a hatch in the top of the fuselage — causing a freezing draught for everyone on board — and "shooting" the altitude of a chosen star with a Mk IX bubble sextant, at the same time noting the time (to

33

Above: Insigne. *Popeye I,* the cartoon insigne applied to Hampden AE238, EA-P of No 49 Squadron at Scampton, 1941.

these were smeared with a sticky yellow concoction called Kilfrost which — allegedly — prevented build-up of ice when such conditions were met. As this stuff also picked up grime, dust etc, the colour usually changed from yellow to a near-black texture, which in no way enhanced the look of our machines.

'Our aircraft then were fitted with Lorenz radio-assisted approach systems, wherein a drift to port of the correct approach line produced the letter "A" in Morse in the headphones, whilst a drift to starboard produced the letter "N"; these two letters being merged into a continuous note on a correct approach. Two markers, an Inner and Outer, indicated distance from the airfield. The indicators were visual as well as audio. We had an Airspeed Oxford at Coningsby fitted with Lorenz for practice approaches, with a Sgt Clark — who had completed his initial tour of ops — as the instructor. The twin aerials stretching from the tailplane to the fuselage in my time were "Top Secret" and all enquiries about their specific purpose were frowned upon. All very hush-hush, but as a matter of fact these were simply part of the IFF system which identified our aircraft on the home radar as "friendly" rather than "hostile". The IFF set on board had a detonator built in which would explode if a press button in the cockpit was pushed in the case of any forced landing in enemy territory. IFF was switched on when approaching the UK on any return trip.

'We were also equipped with R/T sets for talking direct to the control tower. These had a range of about ten miles and were very useful when returning to base after any flight. Coningsby's call-sign was "Jessop". A lot of the bombs we were using were from old stockpiles. Many were 500-pounders, rusty-looking and with the year of manufacture stamped on them — 1918! The 250-pounders we often carried slung outboard under the wings once the main bomb compartment was full. All the squadron had their own individual insignia and crests, with a small bomb added for each operational trip completed. The insigne on my aircraft was the "speedbird" of Imperial Airways, because I'd served with Imperial Airways as an aircrew radio officer on their Empire flying boat fleet before the war.

'In December 1941 chronic sinusitis and a medical board grounded me. By then I'd completed 28 sorties, two short of a first operational tour. Between my arrival at Finningley in December 1940 and departure from Coningsby in December 1941. I had seen No 106 Squadron grow from about six to eighteen crews. After treatment in 1942 and rehabilitation, I was posted to Flying Training Command, in which I served for the rest of the war, being commissioned in 1944.'

the nearest second), thence taking the relative data out of the tables and plotting a position line. We used astro once or twice by getting shots of Polaris which gave a quick check on latitude, but generally it was left to the "keen types" to experiment with. Over Germany we had to rely heavily on map-reading at night. In the case of Bremen or Hamburg or similar targets on or near the coastline there was obviously little difficulty, but in other areas not assisted by natural features and deep inside Germany, small, relatively flak-free targets were awkward to pick out; especially if there were no lakes, rivers or canals in the vicinity to help pinpoint an exact location. Reflection of moonlight on waterways was always a good landmark.

'Of the peculiarities of the Hampden, there were two items in the take-off drill which I've never forgotten. First, when the flaps had to be lowered to 25 degrees for some obscure reason, the starboard flap always came down much quicker than the port. In order to equalise flap positions the starboard engine had to be revved up a bit when lowering flaps so that the slipstream would hold back the starboard flap slightly as it came down. Also on take-off, the Hampden tended to develop a nasty swing to starboard and, in order to get a trouble-free take-off run, when opening the throttles it was better to lead slightly with the starboard throttle which tended to neutralise the incipient swing. Our aircraft were not fitted with any de-icing equipment on the wing leading edges, so

Vignettes

Roy 'Andy' Anderson joined No 83 Squadron in late September 1940 at the start of his operational career, but was more fortunate than most 'sprog' pilots on the unit in having more than 100 hours solo in his logbook already from his prewar RAFO service. On 15 October 1940, along with Flt Lt D. W. F. Barker (pilot), Plt Off Fleming and Sgt Evans, he was in one of 12 Hampdens sent to bomb a German target, in Hampden X2901. In the event his crew was one of seven which bombed the Dortmund-Ems Canal, a secondary objective. As with all 'new' pilots then, Andy was required to act as navigator in his early sorties, to gain experience. He remembers:

'We lost one engine on return to base — the prop did in fact leave us halfway across the North Sea — but the remaining engine brought us back to within sight of the English coast, then it decided to give up the struggle. Luckily it was a fairly calm night with a good moon, but bloody cold. The skipper, "Colonel" Barker, made a first-class belly-landing in the sea some distance from the beach, and after the initial drenching we prepared to abandon the aircraft. The dinghy was launched and one by one we fell or clambered into it, all except Barker who elected to jump into the water with the intention of swimming behind the dinghy and pushing it towards shore. Obviously this was a good

Below: **Off-duty. Flt Lt Roy Anderson (far left) and Guy Gibson (far right), with wives and friends at a local race meeting, 1940.**
Wg Cdr R. Anderson DFC

idea but regrettably he was somehow washed round the end of the Hampden and managed to get his big toe stuck between the elevators! After extricating said member, and once the air in the immediate vicinity had become slightly less blue due to the intensity of his language, he paddled himself round to the dinghy and started to push us away from the aircraft. For a moment he began to tread water, only to find he could stand up — the water hardly reached up to his waist. The laughter and relief may be well imagined, and the other two inmates clambered out and pushed us gently but firmly to shore.

'As the tide was flooding, the Hampden, which in deeper water would have sunk by then, began to follow us like a well-trained pet dog, bouncing on the sandy bottom with each small wave. When at last the dinghy, contents, pushers and the Hampden reached dry land, our immediate concern was to rouse someone to lead us across the beach which would bound to be mined. This proved more of a problem than we would have thought, though in fairness to those on guard it must be remembered that our approach had been practically noiseless, having no engines. The only thing they could have heard would have been the "Colonel's" blastings about his toe predicament. Shouting had no response, and in desperation the air gunner retrieved the Very Pistol and, with permission, fired it, though whether it was the "colour of the day" history doesn't relate. It had the desired effect and in due course we were escorted across the mine field by a not-too-confident Army NCO, who told us afterwards he was quite sure we were Jerries.

'At last, cold and wet, we arrived at a bungalow, the HQ of the Company guarding that stretch of coast, a brew of hot tea duly arrived and tea had never tasted so good. We learnt we were at Southwold on the Norfolk-Suffolk border where, luckily for us, the beach shelves very slowly. After interrogation by the Army, the local police, and some big-shot retired naval officer — we never found out quite what the latter was, something in coastal defence we gathered — we were finally driven off to Martlesham Heath, and hence from there back to Scampton by Anson. On arrival in the Mess we were inspected by certain members who wanted to ensure we all now had webbed feet . . .

Left: Aircrew transport was hardly luxurious in February 1941; exemplified by these crew members of No 83 Squadron at Scampton about to be taken to their aircraft dispersal sites. Note contemporary flying clothing 'fashions' — a mixture of Sidcot overall suits and Irvin 'Parasuits'.

Left: Stalwarts of No 83 Squadron, summer 1940. Back row, from left: Harrison; Sylvester; Craig; Kernaghan; Guy Gibson; Johnson; Haydon. Seated, from left: A. R. Mulligan DFC; J. A. 'Jamie' Pitcairn-Hill DFC; E. H. Ross DFC. The latter three were part of the formation which bombed the Dortmund-Ems Canal on 12/13 August 1940 — the sortie which resulted in the award of Bomber Command's first VC to Flt Lt Roderick Learoyd of No 49 Squadron. Of these 10 pilots, only three survived the war.
Wg Cdr R. Anderson DFC

'During the winter 1940-41 we seemed to receive regular attention from a certain Junkers Ju88 which did a Cook's Tour of five Group stations in the Lincoln area, shooting up aircraft, bombing aerodromes and generally making life a misery. I say a "certain Ju88" because one night a machine gun crew (I believe of No 83 Squadron) managed to shoot down a Ju88 which crashed on the perimeter, after which we were virtually left alone. [Shot down 14 May 1941; Lt Hanning buried Scampton churchyard.] At Scampton at this time we had a particularly enthusiastic Aerodrome Defence Officer who, as soon as there was a Red warning, became very much "in command". On one such occasion, when our friend in the Ju88 was being even more unpleasant than usual, and had just dropped a stick of bombs hitting No 49 Squadron's hangar and offices; the Defence Officer was in full cry. After the bombing he staggered back to the Mess, his face and tunic covered in blood, and, naturally, we all thought he'd been hit. The MO was fetched and the rest of us gathered round full of sympathy to hear the hero's story . . . only to learn that he had been the only "casualty", and that the cause of the "wound" now being dressed was the result of running flat out into a brick wall during the bombing!

'One experience which might have ended in disaster, but in fact had moments of high comedy, occurred on 11 February 1941 when we were returning from a trip to Bremen in Hampden AD734, during which our radio had been put out of action. The weather was ideal until we reached the Dutch coast, when a sea fog blotted out everything. This fog was unbroken the whole way across the North

Left: Cheerful bunch of No 83 Squadron posing for the Press at Scampton, circa February 1941.

Below: Hampden AE196, EQ-M, of No 408 (Goose) Squadron RCAF at Syerston on 12 August 1941. On 13 December 1941 this aircraft was with No 44 Squadron and in action over Brest, piloted by Wg Cdr S. T. Misselbrook DSO and was shot down by flak, killing its crew.
Public Archives of Canada

Sea and, to our dismay, showed no signs of clearing when our ETA at the English coast was well overdue. We did in due course pick up a ground station on R/T, but even circling we lost contact before being able to fix our position.

'I decided to go down a low as possible to see if we could pick up anything that would help us find out if we were still over land, and as we were getting short of fuel we lost height in a very flat power glide. We entered the fog ceiling and almost immediately there

was an explosion, the aircraft lurched, and I promptly climbed up out of the murk. As we emerged into the moonlight we noticed a number of barrage balloons doing the same thing, one of which we must have hit in the fog. Having reached a reasonable height, I set "George" on a westerly course and we all baled out.

'In due course I reached the fog layer and as I sailed through it I almost immediately saw a number of houses, and proceeded to land on the roof of one of them. I must have slithered down and hit my head on something, probably a fence, for I was knocked out for a minute. I then discovered that I had a badly-cut head, but otherwise was in one piece. After shouting at the top of my voice — not a popular pastime — windows opened and I was told in no uncertain terms to "Belt up and go back to bed!" At last I convinced the tenants of the house in whose garden I was standing that I needed help, when at last he and his good lady decided to unbolt the door and let me in. No two people could then have been kinder. He and I shared his last cigarette over several cups of tea, during which time I learned we had arrived at Birmingham.

'I made my way to the local police station, where the whole crew were eventually united. The police were more than kind but insisted that we be medically inspected at the Birmingham General Hospital. There, the doctor in charge — a rather formidable female — was a trifle terse, thinking, I imagine, we'd been on some drunken orgy in the city; we did look a pretty motley crew. However, once the facts were explained there were no more problems. I had to have a few stitches, and the air gunner's foot received attention, otherwise the only casualty was the aircraft. The navigator, Flt Lt Badcock, was absolutely sure his matrimonial prospects had been ruined, as his parachute harness had been a loose fit — even the detailed examination carried out by the lady doctor failed to completely satisfy him that all was well. In due course we arrived back at Lincoln by train, pretty weary, but new members of the Caterpillar Club.'

Flt Lt A. H. Gould DFC, a New Zealand-born pilot who had joined the RAF in March 1938, was skipper of one of six Hampdens despatched on 20 July 1940 to Wilhelmshaven, ostensibly to bomb the battleship *Tirpitz*, then nearing completion. Detailed to bomb from 'low level', in fact only three Hampdens even reached the target, and all three were shot down:
'The first hits we received came from destroyers anchored in the harbour when we were about half a mile from the shore. From then on the Hampden was hit continually all

the way to the target — both engines, part of the wings and fuselage were on fire before we passed over the first wharves. My navigator released our bombs as we approached the battleship. Flames lit up buildings and assisted me to clear masts and gantries. As soon as level ground appeared I pulled everything back to come down on what appeared to be a beach. It turned out to be mud flats exposed by the low tide. Our rear gunner was killed and the navigator thrown through the nose of the aircraft. We three survivors were challenged a few minutes later and captured.'

Another New Zealander, Flt Lt I. C. Kirk, was a Hampden navigator, and was returning from an attack on Mannheim on the night of 2 September 1940:
'It was about midnight and we were flying at about 11,000 feet between Liege and Maastricht when the aircraft was suddenly caught in the beams of many searchlights. Before our pilot could dive clear we were attacked by a Messerschmitt night fighter. The first bursts put our gunners out of action, both mortally wounded; a second attack smashed the controls and set the port engine and fuel tanks on fire. I was wounded in the head and momentarily dazed. On coming to I tried the intercom but got no reply. I attempted to crawl up to help the pilot, thinking he was wounded or dead, but found this impossible even though I used all my strength against what seemed to be a mass of twisted metal and broken wires. The Hampden was now lurching wildly, so groping my way to the escape hatch I dived out. The air seemed buoyant and as I slowed down I saw the Hampden crash and burst into flames. Unknown to me the captain had been thrown out and he had no recollection of pulling his ripcord, only of landing in a ploughed field with his chute opened enough to break his fall. My own had opened cleanly and I landed in a tree. Scrambling down I threw my gear under a bridge, and failing to find any sign of the others, optimistically set off westwards, steering by the stars. Just before dawn a Dutch farmer caught up with me as I limped along. He took me to his home but just as I was about to wash the blood from my head, a German patrol surprised us and took me prisoner.'

Sqn Ldr John van Puyenbroek trained on Hampdens at 14 OTU, Cottesmore from January to May 1941, before commencing operations with No 207 Squadron on Manchesters:
'Whilst at 14 OTU a Manchester crashed nearby and the crew were brought into the Sergeants' Mess late at night; one member was a neighbour of mine from "digs" in Tooting. One of the Vultures (engines) had

caught fire soon after take-off from Waddington and all the crew except the rear gunner had managed to bale out. He said to me, "Never let yourself get posted to Manchesters" — and a couple of months later I was walking through the gates of "Waddo" to join No 207. That night a land mine was dropped over the airfield but missed and hit Waddington Church. A couple of days later we were called out at dawn by a raid warning, and an intruder dropped bombs which killed a couple of WAAFs and three NCOs in the next bomb shelter and two NAAFI girls in a direct hit on the NAAFI building.

'My first operational flight in a Manchester should have been on 22 June 1941, but the pilot, Flg Off Withers, objected to my lack of operational experience and at the last minute I was dropped from his crew. They were aboard Manchester L7314, "Y" which was shot down by a Beaufighter over Northampton. On my birthday, 27 June, I was in charge of the funeral party at Nottingham for the mid-upper gunner who had taken my place . . . On my second trip, to Dusseldorf on 29 June, our starboard engine caught fire over Heligoland Bight and we staggered home on one engine. My friend's warning now had more than a measure of truth! My operational experience of Manchesters in all included 13 ops sorties and one crash. The latter was in L7300, piloted by Plt Off Bill Hills DFM and navigator Warrant Officer 'Goldie' Goldstraw DFC. On 23 November 1941, with the same crew, plus two ground defence officers and the NCO in charge of engines, it suffered a double engine failure and crashed into Fiskerton quarry lake, near Lincoln, and the skill and experience of Bill Hills saved us from almost certain death. It was a Sunday afternoon and a local angling society was dispersed around the periphery of the lake when we dropped in unannounced . . .'

Manchester Moments

On 1 November 1940, No 207 Squadron was reformed as a first-line unit, and seven days later its personnel began assembling at Waddington. Just two days later its first operational aircraft was delivered from No 6 MU, Brize Norton — an Avro Manchester, L7279; the first example of this bomber to enter RAF operational service. Indeed, No 207's terms of reference were to introduce Manchesters to the ops scene, and by the close of that year the unit had at least eight Manchesters on charge, and by 24 February 1941 could muster a total of 18 aircraft. That same date saw six of the squadron's Manchesters make the type's first war sorties — a hastily-mounted raid against a reported 'Hipper' class cruiser in Brest harbour. All six managed to return to base, but one (L7284) crashed on landing back at Waddington due to faulty hydraulics — the ominous beginning of a dispiriting saga of technical failures and faults which were to dog the Manchester throughout its relatively brief fighting career. From this date until the Manchesters' final

operations — the third of 'Butch' Harris's 1,000-bomber raids, against Bremen on 25/26 June 1942 — a total of 202 Manchesters were actually built and delivered to the RAF. In that period nearly 40% were lost on operations, while a further 25% were written-off in crashes, accidents and unexplained technical failures.

On operations Manchesters flew a total of 1,269 individual sorties, almost equally by day and by night, and released 1,826 tons of high explosive bombs on enemy objectives, apart from undertaking 221 'Gardening' trips, and an uncounted tonnage of incendiary stores. the chief cause of the Manchester's failures lay in its power plants — twin Rolls-Royce Vulture X-Inline engines, which at the time of the aircraft's conception in 1936-37 were a new design, yet to be thoroughly developed and tested. The Vulture was, in effect, an unhappy 'marriage' of two sets of cylinder blocks from RR Peregrine engines, mounted on a common crankcase with a 90-degree angle between the

Below: Manchester L7427, OL-Q, 'Queenie' of No 83 Squadron, 1942. It was destined to be lost on its 15th operation, over Hamburg on 8/9 April 1942, with its captain Plt Off Morphett and his crew, Plt Off Lovegrove, Flt Sgts Hutchinson and Salter, and Sgts Williams, Risk, and Gellately. At one period L7427 was coded OL-J.

blocks, giving it an 'X' cross-sectional appearance. Initial factory testing in 1939 quickly convinced the Avro design team that the Vultures were not going to live up to expectations, and alternative power plants were immediately considered. Of the latter, the most significant proposal was for a four-engined version, to be titled the Manchester III, utilising four Rolls-Royce Merlin engines, mounted in an extended wing. This proposal was first committed to paper in September 1939, and bore eventual fruit on 9 January 1941. On that day the prototype 'Manchester III' — or Lancaster, as it was then named — made its first-ever flight from Woodford; the 'father' of 7,377 Lancasters to be built ultimately. Thus, with all its defects and operation failures, the Manchester has a permanent niche in RAF annals — from it came the finest heavy bomber to be flown by the RAF during the years 1939-45.

To the unfortunate crews of 5 Group squadrons tasked with operating Manchesters in 1941-42, however, the 'poten-tial' of the design was by no means apparent. It was, in the succinct phrasing of one veteran Manchester skipper, 'a right cow'... Chief among the crews' complaints was the failure of the type to produce a worthwhile operating altitude — due solely to the lack of real power in its Vulture engines — thereby making every sortie a case of running a gauntlet of flak and night fighters with little alternative for the crew but to grin and bear it. Jack Bushby was one such crew member, an air gunner who had originally joined No 601 Squadron of the Auxiliary Air Force as an aircraft hand in the piping days of peace, and eventually achieved his personal ambition to become air crew:

'When I joined No 4 Manchester Course at 25 OTU, Finningley in September 1941, I was fresh from gunnery school and, as yet, too inexperienced to realise what I and many others were in for. No doubt by that time the experiences of 5 Group squadrons already operating Manchesters had been duly passed to higher authority, but if this was so, that august body of policy-makers never said a word to me about it ... which was understandable, I suppose, since it would hardly have been conducive to high morale to learn that the aircraft on which one was about to commence one's operational career was turning out to be a stinker ... !

'In the event it was almost three months later before our course really got to grips with the beast. Up until then the OTU training exercises had been carried out on Wellingtons, and not until the final phase, in E Flight, did one actually commence real Manchester flying. This took place from Bircotes, a grass airfield near Bawtry, south of Finningley, and it was there that I got my first close-up look, inside and out. As an air gunner, my prime area of interest was the turrets and armament. The rear turret was acceptable and, in some respects, an improvement on that of the Wellington. But that mid-upper turret ...! There and then I swore they would never get me into it, short of a direct order. The Manchester mid-upper turret was the Frazer-Nash Mk VII, but was popularly referred to as the "Botha" turret, since its main application up until then had been in that similarly ill-fated aircraft, the Blackburn Botha. Fitted with two .303in Brownings, its upper portion above the fuselage was a pointed egg-shape with a flattened rear surface in which latter were incorporated two tiny, hinged, emergency escape doors. Access to this dorsal turret from the fuselage was not easy, to say the least, and a hurried exit by this route would have taken so long as not to matter anyway. Hence the above-fuselage doors. I never heard of these ever being used in flight, and the only time I tried it on the ground,

wearing an Irvin jacket, I stuck fast — and I'm not particularly bulky.

'As on the later Lancaster mid-upper, two arms ending in rollers and linked to the gun elevating mechanism protruded from the outside and followed the contour of an external ramp; the whole arrangement being officially christened GTI — Gun Travel Interrupter — and a necessary precaution to prevent gunners shooting off their own tailplanes and rudders. The wings and forward fuselage were similarly protected by this device.

'Our flying in E Flight, 25 OTU proceeded without incident and we notched up a score or so hours before noticing anything peculiar about Manchesters. Not, that is, until our very last flight on New Year's Day 1942, before moving on to 83 Squadron and operations the next day. This flight was meant to be an innocuous hour's circuits and bumps, chiefly for the pilot's benefit, and utilising dark glasses and a new sodium lamp flare

Above left: Up front. The skipper's cockpit in a Manchester. *IWM*

Left: Interior. Inside a Manchester, looking towards the rear turret.

Top: Manchester R5833, OL-N 'Nuts', No 83 Squadron, Scampton on 8 April 1942. Crew here are, from left: Sgt Jack Bushby (AG); Plt Off Billings RNZAF (Nav); Sgt Dodsworth (W/Op/AG); Sgt Baines (W/Op/AG); Sgt Williams (2/Pilot); Warrant Officer Whitehead DFM (Captain). Motto on nose is in Welsh, *Ar Hyd y Nos* (appropriately, 'All through the night'). This aircraft was next used by No 50 Squadron and lost in action over Ile de Quiberone on a mining sortie, 5/6 June 1942.
J. Bushby

Above: Manchester R5784 of No 50 Squadron in May 1942. Crew, from left are: Sgt S. A. Gawler (AG); AC Rodger; Sgt Welford (W/Op/AG); Sgt G. Murtough (AG); Plt Off T. B. 'King' Cole DFC; Plt Off P. W. Rowling (Nav). *T. B. Cole DFC*

path as a sort of makeshift nightflying-in-daylight experiment. Two student pilots and an experienced second-tour instructor were up at the sharp end, happily carrying out their exercise. We crew members, somewhat superfluous on this local jaunt in daylight, were continuing the previous evening's four-handed cribbage tournament on the main spar casing of L7431.

'The wheels had just been lowered for the umpteenth approach when there came an audible bang — and motley pieces of the port engine began to shoot past our side windows. Up in the cockpit there was a moment of wild confusion, with arms flying out punching feathering buttons in all directions and pilots squirming over and round each other, exchanging seats. Once installed in the left-hand seat the intstructor yelled back something about not being able to hold her and to hang on! Even with our minimal load a single engine overshoot proved impossible and, skipping the intervening heart-stopping

minutes, that flight finished in a crashing, slithering belly-landing across a wet ploughed field; the wild slide being arrested by a sturdy oak tree just as it ran out of impetus. Fortunately no one was injured, and considering that with the loss of one engine a Manchester's sole inclination was to adopt the gliding angle of a streamlined brick, the instructor handled the situation extremely well.

'One disturbing characteristic of Vulture engines, apart from their unreliability and failure to deliver the "urge", was the long, brilliant comet trail of fiery red sparks which they threw out even when running normally. At night these were visible for miles and all kinds of dodges were tried to trap and suppress these trails, without success. No German night-fighter needed radar when Manchesters were about, and to my mind this might have accounted for more than a few being easily stalked and shot down.

'About mid-fuselage the Manchester

45

carried a monumental structure looking not unlike a scaled-down Wurlitzer organ and known officially as a triple flare chute. The centre chute was for the high candlepower photo-flash, while the two side chutes were for any other pyrotechnic device needing to be launched. The bottom of each chute was sealed off with a sliding tin cover actuated from the cockpit, which when slid back allowed the flare or flash to drop down and out. Some of our OTU exercises called for the release of an aluminium sea-marker which, when it hit the water, spread a sizeable patch of fine aluminium powder on the sea surface, thus forming a target for gunners to aim at. It was only a question of time before the incidence of Murphy's Law and, sure enough, one day someone let the marker go before the bottom trap was open, and it functioned inside the aircraft. On landing, the crew emerged coated in silver from head to foot, while the interior of the Manchester was like a department store Christmas grotto.

'These side chutes were also used for pushing out bundles of propaganda leaflets with which the chairborne Ministry of Propaganda warriors had decided the war would be won. I found out about these the hard way. The first time I filled the chute with bundles of bumf and the trap was operated, the resulting hurricane of slipstream draught back up the chute caused the lot to be "returned to sender". The dark interior then became a mass of flapping, whirling paper, plastering itself over me and everything else. As "Chiefy" remarked caustically after we

Above: Going over — a Manchester (triple-fin variant) en route to Germany early 1942.

Right: Waiting. Scene at Waddington Control Tower in 1941 as senior officers await the return of an operational raid. From left: Flt Lt Hobson (Air Traffic Controller); Wg Cdr Burton-Gyles (No 44 Squadron); Wg Cdr K. P. Lewis (Station Cdr); and Sqn Ldr Laborne (Senior Air Traffic Controller). Burton-Gyles became commander of the newly-forming No 408 Squadron RCAF at the end of 1941. *IWM*

Above: L7477, QR-N of No 61 Squadron at Woolfox Lodge after operations on 12 February 1942 against the German capital ships *Scharnhorst* and *Gneisenau* during their famed 'Channel Dash'. Other damage necessitated replacement of the tail unit. *C. Bowyer*

Left: Bullseye. Flak damage to Manchester R5830, OL-L of No 83 Squadron, on the night of 29 March 1942.

Far right: **Bomb train of 2,000lb bombs being tractored alongside Manchester L7385, OL-C of No 83 Squadron, April 1942. The insigne painted under C-Charlie's cockpit was a Lion rampant — a remarkable coincidence in view of 5 Group's eventual official badge motif.** *Central Press*

landed, it looked like " . . . a blitzed toilet". After this incident we just bunged them out still in their bales in the hope that a solid bundle would descend on a Nazi head and do that much good at least. Since a crew member had to devote several minutes to this task, I frequently speculate on how many bombers thus deprived of half of their rearward outlook might have been caught napping by night fighters during such a futile exercise.

'No 83 Squadron began Manchester operations with an easy one to Boulogne on the night of 28 January 1942. All four aircraft returned safely but, after landing, an exclamation from a rigger drew my attention to the central stabiliser of L7423 — a triple-finned Manchester — and in the light of his torch I saw that the whole fabric covering had mysteriously disappeared during flight, leaving only the bare metal skeleton. A few days later an A Flight Manchester, ambling sedately round the Scampton circuit preparatory to landing, nonchalantly shed its port fin *and* rudder before our astonished gaze. A somewhat asymmetric and decidedly shaky landing was made and the crumpled bits retrieved from a few fields away. And it was on a cold February afternoon that we taxied back to dispersal after a night-flying test and stopped engines. As the ginormous 7ft 6in blades of the port propeller swung to rest there was a musical tinkling sound. A fitter removed the spinner hub and, after investigation, reported that the whole reduction gear had seized and that several propeller retaining bolts had already sheared. Five minutes earlier and we would have anticipated that Apollo 13 crew's "Hey! We've got a problem!" . . .

'Almost every target selected during the winter months of early 1942 was a heavily defended one. We went to Essen, Bremen, Cologne, Wilhelmshaven and Hamburg — then started all over again. The second-tour pilots soon came to realise grimly that with anything like a respectable bomb load they just could not attack the "Happy Valley" (Ruhr) at any more altitude than they had in the obsolescent Hampdens of their first tours. Meanwhile, German flak and night fighter defences had increased in quantity and greatly improved in accuracy; thus at 10 to 12,000 feet we were nicely in the preferred bracket of heavy stuff, yet not out of reach of the light stuff. On one night, Hamburg-bound, we found that our Manchester, R5830, would not even make 10,000 feet without serious overheating of the already suspect engines. To solve this problem two of the six 1,000lb bombs aboard were smartly jettisoned over the Frisians, and with a reduced load of 4,000lb a reasonable cylinder-head temperature could be maintained at pre-

cisely 11,000 feet. Then there was the occasion when a CSU (Constant Speed Unit) gave up the ghost over Essen. The resulting howl must have terrified the ground defences — it certainly shook us.

'On 12 February came the escape of the *Scharnhorst* and *Gneisenau*, known irreverently as "Salmon and Glukstein" to all 1942 bomber crews. All day we stood by but were not ordered off. Night fell and we were stood down. The Mess bar had just opened when my crew were called to the crew room by the Tannoy and there told that we had been "selected" for the dubious honour of flying across the cold, dark, winter North Sea at low level to drop sea mines in the predicted path of the German ships a mile or two off the German coast. It was touch and go whether we would make it in time, but make it we did. History records that at about that time, and in that place, one of the ships was so damaged by a mine that she had to put in to port and then remained there for the rest of the war. So perhaps our journey was necessary. On the way back, at only two or three thousand feet over the icy oggin, seven hearts jumped into seven mouths when the second pilot reported the port revolutions counter going off the clock at the wrong end. With computer-like rapidity seven minds had already worked out that with the height loss to be expected immediately as one engine failed, and even if she would fly on the other one, we would be several hundred feet below the waves before the situation was stabilised. Fortunately it turned out to be a case of a duff instrument, but never was an engine's note listened to more keenly or with such rapt attention than in Manchester L7464 that night.

'Other crews had their moments too, of course. Although on the face of it the Manchester problem was simply that of an under-powered design suffering from poor performance, peculiar things used to happen to the airframe and equipment. Revs counters would suddenly offer wild and impossible readings, like the night we took off with — according to the panel — 2,850rpm on port and 4,500rpm on starboard. Gyro repeaters and artificial horizons, without warning, took off in erratic rotations round the dials; the intercom would become swamped with screaming gremlins and all communications become impossible. Even "George" (automatic pilot) had occasional fits of gay abandon, trying to perform aerobatics on the way out and back. And there was the 44 Squadron Manchester at Waddington which shed a leading edge on take-off and careered into parked aircraft, somewhat to the detriment of the war effort. With all due respect, later generations of air crews never knew how interesting life could be

Above: **Changing to Lancs. No 83 Squadron crew at Scampton on 14 May 1942, about to board their new Lancaster. Note Manchester in background. Crew included from left: Unknown; Flt Sgt 'Mush' Corfield; Flt Sgt 'Joe' Taylor, sporting his pre-1939 'cheesecutter' hat which he insisted on wearing through two operational tours; while far right is Flt Sgt Kitto.** *J. Bushby*

dodging the Happy Valley flak at eight to nine thousand feet and wondering what was going to fall off next.

'The worst aspect of all this was its effect on morale. No one ever got to the point of actually gibbering with terror every time they saw a Manchester, and corny jokes continued to come thick and fast. Yet beneath all this banter was a lack of confidence in one's equipment; bad enough in any sphere but fatal in war operations. There was a continual niggling worry in the back of many minds that sometime soon, maybe, something was going to go wrong at a critical moment, perhaps with fatal results, which must have affected the ability to make instant and correct decisions. Such was the Manchester's evil reputation that it is a matter of record that Flt Lt "Kipper" Herring, of No 207 Squadron brought his Manchester (L7432, "Z") back from the "Big

City" (Berlin) on one engine, below 1,000 feet all the way, and was awarded an immediate DSO. Unanimous 5 Group opinion was that a decoration was never more richly deserved. Rumour had it that at one point Herring's crew had nothing left to throw overboard but their trousers, and were starting to dismantle the airframe to save an extra pound or two of weight to scrape home across the North Sea.

'In May 1942 I was detached on a gunnery leader's course, having survived — and I select that word deliberately — ten operational trips on Manchesters, with a total of over 100 hours on the type. It was with a feeling of heartfelt relief that I returned at the end of the month to find them gone, replaced by Lancasters, although it was saddening to know that many of them had gone down into the night over Germany, taking with them more than half of the crews alongside whom I had trained at Finningley.'

Low-Level to Augsburg

The introduction of the Avro Lancaster to RAF Bomber Command heralded an era of strategic and tactical bombing offensive against Germany in ever-increasing strength and weight which, in partnership with the escalating day bomber offensive of the American Eighth Air Force, was to finally cripple the heart of Hitler's Nazi empire. Contrary to the oft-repeated legend that the Lancaster resulted from the dismal failure of the Manchester bomber on operations, the conception of a four Merlin-engined version of the embryo Manchester was committed to paper as early as September 1939 — only eight weeks after the first prototype Manchester had made its 'maiden' flight, and a year before the first Manchester was even received by an RAF front-line squadron. The first prototype Lancaster was, in fact, constructed from a standard Manchester airframe (serialled BT308) fitted with extended wings to accommodate four Rolls-Royce Merlin X engines, each of 1,145hp. In this guise it first flew on 9 January 1941 at Woodford, and later that month was sent to Boscombe Down for Service evaluation. With its original Manchester triple-fin tail unit exchanged for the more familiar twin-fin configuration, this Lancaster was then received by No 44 Squadron on 16 September 1941 for crew familiarisation.

Conversion from Manchesters to the Lancaster was relatively simple for No 44 Squadron's crews. The basic fuselage layout, cockpit et al were almost identical. Nevertheless, initial practice flights in Lancasters produced a variety of problems, due mainly to the greater weight and associated handling characteristics of this new, four-engined design. No 44's first operational Lancasters began arriving at Waddington on Christmas Eve, 1941 when L7537, L7538 and L7541 were allocated. If the air crew found a few problems in handling the Lanc, these were relatively small compared to the myriad complexities met by the ground crews in initial maintenance. Servicing manuals were only just being produced for the various skilled trades, and even these were based more on theory than solid experience. In particular the armourers and engine fitters faced a host of fresh situations, yet — as with all operational squadron ground crews — they buckled down to their tasks with huge energy and expertise and solved each problem as it arose. During the working-up period on Lancasters, No 44's crews suffered a series of minor flying and

Below: **The prototype Avro Lancaster, BT308, which was demonstrated to No 44 Squadron crews on 15 September 1941. The squadron then received its first three production Lancs on Christmas Eve, and eventually flew its first Lanc operations on 3 March 1942. Seen in the background here is a Blackburn Roc two-seater of the Fleet Air Arm.** *Hawker-Siddeley Aviation*

Left: Sqn Ldr John Dering Nettleton, wearing the ribbon of his VC, with Sqn Ldr Whitehead DFC.

Below: Flt Lt R. R. 'Nick' Sandford with his pet dog 'Nigger'. In background is Waddington's Watch Tower.

landing accidents, though without fatal casualties, and by 25 January 1942 the crews were warned to stand by for operations. Inclement weather intervened and it was not until 3 March that No 44 Squadron finally blooded the Lancaster on operations — four Lancs taking off for a mine-laying sortie in the Heligoland Bight, from which all returned safely. Five days later, eight of the unit's Lancs were detached to Lossiemouth with orders to prepare for a strike against the German battleship *Tirpitz* (then in Norwegian waters), but in their absence from Waddington two of No 44's aircraft (L7356 and L7366) participated in a bombing raid against Essen on 10 March — the first Lancaster bombing operation. Perhaps inevitably, the first operational loss of a Lancaster followed shortly after, when R5493, skippered by Flt Sgt Warren-Smith, failed to return from a 'Gardening' sortie on 24 March.

While No 44 Squadron had been familiarising itself with the new bombers, a second unit began re-equipment; No 97 Squadron, based at Coningsby, which received its first Lancaster on 14 January 1942, and had a strength of 17 a month later. No 97 made its initial Lancaster operational sorties on 20 March when six crews set out on mine-laying trips, and all six returned; albeit landing back at various airfields, including two crash-landings. Officialdom intended to convert the whole of 5 Group to an all-Lancaster formation, and Nos 207, 61, 83 and 106 Squadrons were, respectively, earmarked for future re-equipment; while

52

Nos 49 and 50 Squadrons continued, at least temporarily, to soldier on with the ill-starred Manchester. In the interim, Nos 44 and 97, each having commenced operations in Lancasters, were to be paired for an operation which was — deservedly — to be called the '...most daring raid of the war'. The vital battle of the Atlantic, upon the outcome of which largely depended Britain's survival, was reaching a crucial stage. All possible aid was needed if the growing German U-boat menace was to be defeated. Accordingly, the newly-installed AOC-in-C of Bomber Command, Arthur Harris — 'Butch' to all his crews — was requested to lay on a bombing raid against a vital factory producing diesel engines for submarines; the MAN (*Maschinenfabrik Augsburg Nürnberg AG*) works near Augsburg in southern Germany. The prospect of such a sortie was breathtaking, involving a round trip of more then 1,000 miles, mostly over enemy-occupied territory. Moreover, such a trip would need to be flown mainly in daylight if accuracy in navigation and actual bombing was to be achieved.

In the second week of April 1942 both Nos 44 and 97 Squadrons' crews were given orders to start practising long-distance formation flights around Britain, ostensibly for obtaining 'endurance data' on the Lancaster, and some emphasis was given to a need for 'low altitude flying'. These 'practice' flights gave rise to general speculation among the crews, most of whom became convinced that 'something special' was on the cards in the very near future, but a tight clamp on secrecy prevented even a clue to just what such an operation might be. Unknown to each other, both squadrons had eight crews selected to continue practising low-level, long-distance flights around the UK in their Lancasters. Finally, on the morning of 17 April, all crews involved were given their briefing — Augsburg, in daylight, that same day. Among the very few men already in the secret was David Penman of No 97 Squadron who, only the day before, had been taken to 5 Group HQ at Grantham, along with Sqn Ldr 'Flap' Sherwood and the Woodhall Spa Station Commander. In Penman's own words:
'When the target was revealed we were shattered; suicide was the common thought. The briefing was, however, very thorough, making use of an excellent scale model of the factory. Emphasis was put on low-level to avoid detection, massive diversionary raids were to be laid on, and little or no AA (flak) was expected at Augsburg... On the 17th briefing was held immediately after lunch with the crews already kitted to go. The scale model was on display and the gasps as the crews entered the room were distinctively audible!

Even though the crews were unaware of the precise target before the briefing, the same morning's airfield activity had already part-prepared them for a 'long run'. Out on the dispersals the Lancasters had been filled with maximum fuel — 2,154 gallons — in itself an indication; while the armourers had been sweating a load of four 1,000lb GP bombs, fitted with 11-second delay detonators, into each of the participating 16 Lancasters. It all added up to a maximum range target. Take-off was schedule for 3.15pm, and at both Woodhall Spa and Waddington eight Lancasters began their pre-take-off checks and engine runs. The actual raiding forces were to be six Lancs from each squadron, each in two vics of three; the remaining pair in each case were simply reserves ready to replace any last-minute 'casualties'. No 44 Squadron's sextet was to lead the raid, under the overall command of Sqn Ldr John Nettleton of No 44, piloting Lancaster R5508, KM-B; while No 97's six aircraft in the rear were led by Sqn Ldr Sherwood in L7573, OF-K. Maintaining a height of about 250 feet, all twelve headed south to Selsey

Below: **Plt Off H. A. P. 'Buster' Peall (centre) with Sgt Peter Rix (left) and Horace Gottlieb, Waddington 1942.**

Bill, then dropped to wave-top height to cross the Channel. Avoidance of detection was virtually the Lancasters' only hope of survival on the outward leg. There was no fighter escort, although a force of 30 Boston bombers and almost 800 RAF fighters were simultaneously undertaking diversionary raids away from the Lancasters' route in the hope of drawing off any Luftwaffe defenders. If any of the bombers ran into German fighters their sole hope of salvation was a tight formation, relying on a concentrated defence from the combined fire from all gun turrets; though even here Penman's rear gun turret was reported unserviceable before he had crossed the French coast.

By the time the Channel had been crossed Nettleton's front formation of six had pulled ahead of Sherwood's, but the latter made no attempt to catch up; briefing had permitted separate attacks if circumstances so decreed, and Sherwood was highly conscious of the need to preserve fuel on such an extended sortie. Crossing into German-occupied France, the two formations hugged the contours of the ground and received no serious opposition from any ground defences. Nettleton and his two vics of three from No 44 Squadron, drumming across the countryside at no more than 50 feet, had a trouble-free trip until their flightpath skirted the outer boundary of Beaumont le Roger airfield — then their luck ran out. As the bombers appeared a gaggle of Messerschmitt Bf109s and Focke Wulf Fw190s of II Gruppe/Jagdgeschwader 2 'Richthofen' were in various stages of landing after an engagement in the Cherbourg area with some of the RAF's diversionary raids. For a few heartstopping seconds the bomber crews thought that they may not have been spotted, but then several of the German fighters were seen to snap up their already-lowered undercarriages and turn quickly towards the Lancasters. Unescorted, and in broad daylight, there could be only one conclusion for the bombers.

The rear vic of the No 44 Squadron formation was first to be attacked, and the first Lancaster to go was L7565, 'V', skippered by Warrant Officer J. E. Beckett. Hit by a hail of cannon shells from a fighter piloted by Hauptman Heine Greisert, the bomber dived into a clump of trees in a roaring furnace of

Right: **Lancaster B1, L7578, with John Nettleton at the controls, on either 14 or 15 April 1942; the two days he spent practising for the Augsburg raid. Though marked KM-B, it was in another Lanc B-Baker (R5508) that he actually led the Augsburg sortie.** *Hawker-Siddeley Aviation*

flames. Next to go was R5506, 'P', piloted by the Rhodesian veteran Flt Lt 'Nick' Sandford, which was attacked by Feldwebel Bosseckert whose fire set all four Merlins ablaze before the bomber exploded in a giant fireball. The wheeling Luftwaffe fighter pack then gave their undivided attention to L7548, 'T', piloted by Warrant Officer H. V. Crum. Converging in a wide arc from a dozen different directions, they bore in and the interior of 'T-Tommy' became a nightmare of ricochetting bullets. Both the rear and mid-upper gunners shouted that they'd been hit. Then a fire started in the port wing, as Crum fought to retain control. He shouted an order to jettison the bomb load, and Sgt Dedman acted immediately, releasing the four thousand-pounders 'safe'. The lightening of the load made little difference — the shredded and burning bomber wallowed alarmingly as Crum used every ounce of strength to hold her steady. He daren't pull up the nose — the fighters were waiting for just such a move — and therefore decided that he had no alternative but to put the aircraft down, a tactic already agreed prior to take-off. Jerking the nose forward to avoid yet another fighter onslaught, Crum selected a wheat field dead ahead, then closed the throttles. Ploughing through the wheat like some grotesque harvester, the crippled Lancaster eventually came to rest at the field's boundary. Crum's crew quickly abandoned the wreck, then set it afire, split into small parties, and set out to reach unoccupied France. All were eventually caught by the Germans and spent the rest of the war as prisoners. Unbeknown to Crum and his crew, they had been jumped by

Above: **Flt Lt John Garwell DFC, DFM of No 44 Squadron, who was shot down over Augsburg in Lanc R5510 'A' but survived the crash. This sketch was drawn by a fellow-prisoner in Stalag Luft 3, Flt Lt Ley Kenyon DFC, an air gunner.** *L. Kenyon*

Right: **Some of the survivors. From left: Sqn Ldr D. J. Penman DSO, DFC; Sgt D. N. Huntley DFM; Plt Off D. Sands DFC; Brendan Bracken (Minister of Information); Flt Lt B. R. W. 'Darky' Hallowes DFC; Sgt R. P. Irons DFM; Sqn Ldr J. D. Nettleton VC.**

Far right: **The French mass grave for members of Sandford's and Beckett's crews. Other crew members not mentioned on this marker include Beckett, Sgt A. J. Harrison, Flg Off Georie and Flt Sgt Law.**

Unteroffizier Pohl, flying his Bf109, 'Black 7', and Pohl's victory was recorded in the Jagdgeschwader's 'Game Book' as its 1,000th claimed *Luftsieg* of the war to date.

Having disposed of the rear vic of three from the No 44 Squadron formation, the German fighters now started attacks on Nettleton's leading vic. Foremost in the onslaught was Major Oesau, a 100-victory 'ace' officially forbidden to fly on operations, but who had jumped into a fighter and taken off on first sighting the Lancasters, followed closely by his wingman Oberfeldwebel Edelmann. As he closed on the rear of the bombers Oesau selected L7536, 'H', piloted by Warrant Officer G. T. Rhodes, as his target. Closing to within 10 metres, firing all guns and cannons in a withering hail of fire, he watched the bomber's port engines both erupt in flames, quickly followed by a surge of flame from the starboard motors. The stricken Lancaster reared abruptly — '. . . as if in agony . . .' (sic) stalled harshly, plunged straight down, passing between Nettleton and the remaining Lancaster in a vertical dive and missing both by mere inches. Only then did the mass of fighters withdraw; empty fuel tanks and depleted ammunition boxes forcing them to return to base. Though extensively damaged, the two remaining Lancasters — R5510, 'A', skippered by Flg Off J. Garwell DFC, DFM, and Nettleton's 'B-Baker' — continued towards their objective. Reaching Augsburg, both bombers flew straight across their target in close formation, released their bombs, then began the run-out. At that moment Garwell's aircraft staggered as flak tore chunks out of the wings and fuselage. Pluming smoke and flames, the bomber headed down as Garwell put it on the ground as fast as possible before any explosion. Belly-landing, he managed to save the lives of all but three of his crew. Nettleton, the sole survivor, pulled away from the scene and set course for England. By then evening was closing in, thus the gathering night would provide a slim protection as he made for home.

Only minutes behind, Sherwood's No 97 Squadron Lancasters began their final approach to the MAN factory. These had not suffered from the attentions of the Richthofen Geschwader, but now faced highly alerted flak defences around the target. Dave Penman picks up the story at this juncture:

'Rising ground forced us a little higher and then we saw the final turning point, a small lake. At this stage, mindful of the 11-second delay fuses, I had dropped back a little from Sherwood's section, and made one orbit before running in to attack. The river was a very good guide and it all showed up as predicted on the scale model. A column of smoke beyond the target came, presumably, from

Garwell's aircraft, and it was quickly joined by another as Sherwood received a shell through the port tank just behind the inboard engine. Escaping vapour caught fire and as he passed over the target he began to turn left. His port wing struck rising ground and the aircraft exploded in a ball of flame. I was convinced that no one could have survived, and on my return reluctantly told Mrs Sherwood. She would not believe it, and events proved her right. I met him again after the war; he had been thrown, complete with his seat, through the windscreen as the aircraft struck the ground — the only survivor.

'As we ran in at 250 feet tracer shells from light AA on the roofs of the buildings produced a hail of fire and all aircraft were hit. Mycock [Warrant Officer T. J. Mycock DFC in Lanc, R5513, 'P'] on my left received a shell in the front turret which set fire to the hydraulic oil within seconds. The aircraft was a sheet of flame. It reared up and turned right, passing right over my head with its bomb doors fully open, before plunging in to the ground, burning from end to end. A shell ripped the cowling from my port inner, and Deverill [Flg Off E. A. Deverill] received a hit near the mid-upper turret at the same time which started a fire. Despite these distractions we held course, with my front gunner doing his best to reduce the opposition. Ifould, my navigator, was then passing instructions for the bomb run. As he finally called "Bombs gone" we passed over the factory. I increased power and dived as Deverill passed me with one engine feathered and the remaining three flat out. I called him and he asked me to cover his rear as his turrets were out of action. Ours had been unserviceable since the Channel, and as we had no wish to relinquish the navigation, I told him to remain in position.

'Our attack had been close to the planned time of 2020hrs, and as darkness came over we climbed to 20,000ft for a direct run home over Germany. It says much for Deverill's skill that he remained in position until we reached the English coast and finally landed at Woodhall Spa. All surviving crews were grounded on return until after a press conference at the Ministry of Information in London'

John Nettleton, the sole survivor from the first formation, eventually landed at Squires Gate aerodrome, Blackpool, just before 1am, and immediately telephoned his report to Waddington, then asked about the other survivors. Of the 12 aircraft which had set out, only five had returned; of the 85 crew members, 49 were 'missing'. On April 28 the *London Gazette* announced the award of a Victoria Cross to Nettleton, and a flock of DFCs, DFMs and a DSO to the other surviv-

ing crew men. In January 1943 John Nettleton was promoted to Wing Commander and appointed as commander of No 44 Squadron on his return to the operational scene. On the night of 12/13 July he set out to bomb Turin, but failed to return.

Much press and official propaganda was expounded on the 'vast damage' inflicted on the MAN factory, though RAF Intelligence viewing of reconnaissance evidence was less optimistic. Postwar examination of German documents and records show that only 17 of the bombs actually hit any part of the diesel engine works, five of which failed to explode. The remaining dozen bombs caused merely three per cent of the machine tools in the whole plant to be put out of action. Successful or not in its intention, the raid had shown in stark clarity that unescorted, daylight raids — particularly where these sought to exploit the extended range of operations offered by the Lancaster — were potentially disastrous, and could only provide unacceptable and unsustainable casualty rates. It has also exemplified the sheer courage and determination of the 'pioneer' Lancaster crews — an example that was to be embellished in superb fashion by all other Lancaster crews in the remaining years of the war.

Left: Lanc Z-Zulu of No 44
Squadron at Dunholme Lodge in
May 1942 — reputedly
Nettleton's aircraft but this is
unconfirmed.

Below: The wedding reception for
John Nettleton VC and his bride,
Section Officer Betty née
Havelock WAAF, 1 July 1942.

Target Hamburg

Below: Refuelling from an AEC Matador, while nearby lie several Small Bomb Containers (SBCs) of 4lb incendiary bombs awaiting loading once the engine fitters had completed their pre-flight tasks and checks.

Top right: Cpl 'Fergie' Ferguson (right) supervising a bowser fill-up on a No 57 Squadron Lanc at East Kirkby.
H. B. Mackinnon DFC

Below right, centre: Ops' eggs. LACW 'Goldie' Goldthorne (centre) waiting to serve operational crews with their traditional 'hen fruit' meal in East Kirkby's Officers' Mess (No 57 Squadron). *H. B. Mackinnon DFC*

Below far right: Ready to go. Flt Lt 'Micky' Carr RAAF at the controls of Lanc N-Nan, of No 57 Squadron, East Kirkby.

To endure high odds against survival deliberately night after night in the skies over Germany required a unique form of courage. Men, especially young men, do not lightly place their lives in constant jeopardy, particularly in circumstances where death or horrifying mutilation came from an unseen enemy swiftly, without warning, preamble or mercy. Yet another hazard was battle fatigue — the American medical phrase for operational veterans in all fighting services who had reached (or gone beyond) the limits of their mental and physical endurance. It was a condition not uncommon among air crews as they reached the end of their first tour of ops, and more often during second or subsequent tours. Yet to be 'rested' from operations in the middle of a tour was regarded with the all-too human fear of being stigmatised by fellow crew members as 'LMF' (Lack of Moral Fibre) — or, in the vernacular, plain 'yellow'. On the squadrons the tell-tale signs of battle fatigue were classified succinctly as the 'twitch', and conscientious unit medical officers and squadron commanders could often quietly divert such

individuals to more restful occupations with no stigma being attached to the record of the crew member concerned. Too often however, men on the verge of cracking went unnoticed until some crisis exploded and threw the unfortunate flier into stark relief against the background of 'normality'.

In a majority of cases men hid their natural fears successfully from outside view, and completed full tours of duty before any reaction became plain. In so many cases this inevitable reaction then took a relatively heavy toll of nerves and body; long submerged fears surfaced and found expression in myriad ways later, even leading in no few cases to a complete breakdown in health or mind. Stan Williams — the name is a pseudonym at the insistence of the contributor here — was older than the average air crew member at 32 years of age, was married with two children, when he first volunteered for flying duties with the RAF in late 1939. His civilian job as a radio fitter led to his acceptance for training as a wireless operator/air gunner and, after the delays and rather haphazard instructional courses avail-

able in 1939-40, he eventually joined his first operational squadron in early 1941, flying Hampdens and, later, Manchesters. His first operational sortie — a 'soft' mining trip to the Dutch coast zone — seemed to set the pace for all subsequent ops. Over the dropping zone his Hampden was hit by flak which sliced chunks out of one engine, damaged the hydraulic system and killed the bomb aimer up front. The return trip at bare altitude across the North Sea ended in an horrendous crash-landing.

The next few ops seemed (to Williams) to prove that he had a jinx on his broad shoulders; virtually every trip resulted in return journeys in damaged and scarred aircraft. A change from Hampdens to Manchesters did nothing to improve his 'luck' — if anything Manchester operations appeared to offer even less chance of ever surviving his first tour. In his own words: 'The Manchester was a pig, and whoever put them in operational squadrons needed shooting . . .' However, survive he did and, in early 1942, Stan was posted to a wireless school as an instructor. Even his limited flying here continued the run of bad luck, with two minor crashes in Oxfords from which he emerged uninjured but definitely 'shaken'. When, in August 1942, Williams was recalled for a second operational tour, his feelings were distinctly mixed. His posting was to a Lancaster unit, which brightened his outlook; at least this time he'd be in a 'decent bomber' (sic). His first few days with the squadron were filled mainly with getting used to the Lancaster — no great problem for an ex-Manchester crew man — and getting to know his fellow crew members. 'The skipper,

like me, was a second-tour type, but the rest were sprogs just beginning ops. They seemed so bloody young to me at first, though whether this was due to the ten or so years age difference, or my previous experience, I couldn't really say.'

His first Lancaster sortie proved to be a 'milk run' — straight into the target without much fuss, a good bombing run, and a trouble-free trip home. Williams' natural anxieties about resuming operations were somewhat calmed, and the next four sorties — with one minor exception, equally trouble-free — seemed to confirm that his first-tour jinx had finally left him. The sixth operation was to Hamburg. He recalls:

'We — my crew — were due for a few days' leave next morning and were in something of a holiday mood prior to briefing for Hamburg. The briefing was straightforward and the target appeared to offer nothing untoward. I was neither pessimistic nor optimistic — it was one more place to clobber, no more, no less. My job now was almost exclusively radio operator, as we had two straight AGs for the mid-upper and rear turrets, though all three of us could interchange places if required. We left base shortly before midnight and climbed as high as possible — our skipper always ignored "recommended heights" and preferred the relative safety of altitude, rather than sticking with the main stream's height. I imagine this idiosyncrasy was the result of some incident in his first tour, but none of us cared to argue with him, preferring to place our complete trust in his hands — he was the boss. It was a bright moonlit night and on the outward legs we saw no other Lancs anywhere near us —

Above: W/Op. Plt Off C. Calton, a wireless operator of No 619 Squadron, in February 1944, fully kitted for a sortie and at his 'desk'. *IWM*

Right: Nav. Flg Off P. Ingleby, navigator, also of No 619 Squadron, photographed at his table on 14 February 1944. He was destined to die over Germany. *IWM*

an eery feeling of being quite alone in the sky which never did much for my morale. We crossed the enemy coast on track and time and made the last turn towards the target — then all hell broke loose.

'The first I was aware of anything going on was a blast of noise and metal above and behind my seat, which made me jump about a foot in the air. A Jerry fighter had caught the gunners napping and put a burst of cannon straight through our mid-section. The skipper immediately dropped the nose, banked violently, then screwed upwards. The intercom became a babble of voices, each yelling instructions, until the skipper shouted "Belt up!" and then asked the gunners for evasion tactics. The rear gunner reported no sighting of the Jerry but nothing came from the mid-upper, a 19-year old Cockney lad whom I'd invited home on leave next day because he had no real home — an ex-Barnardo boy. The skipper called him again and, on getting no reply, told me to take a look at him. I climbed over the main spar and made my way aft to the turret. The boy's booted feet were dangling loosely above me and as I looked up I felt liquid pouring on to my face. At first I thought it was hydraulic oil, but it was blood. The gunner had obviously been hit badly, and it took a lot of effort to disentangle him from the turret and get him down on to the fuselage floor. Then I got my first good look at him.

'One arm was virtually shot off at the shoulder, while that side of his face and helmet was an unrecognisable mess in the dim light available. I remember my immediate reaction was, "How the hell can I apply a tourniquet to a missing arm?" — a stupid idea. I plugged in to the intercom and reported to the skipper, who said, "OK. Take over the turret if it's still working. Taffy (to the navigator), take care of the gunner for now". I waited until the navigator arrived and his reaction on seeing my blood-covered face and gear was to ask, "God Almighty, you too?" I reassured him, then climbed in to the mid-upper turret. Most of the perspex was gone, shattered, but the controls brought response so I settled down behind the Brownings and told the skipper. Rotating 360-degrees carefully, I could see no sign of any fighter, but kept traversing, quartering the upper sky methodically. Nothing in sight. My thoughts were mixed, thinking of that poor kid below with half a head — what a way to go. It was bloody cold, sitting there without cover from the slipstream, and I felt the blood on my face — the kid's blood — caking hard and stiffening up my facial muscles, making it difficult to speak or even breathe properly. I thought of my wife and her beauty mud-packs, and almost giggled.

'Soon we were approaching the target, Hamburg, and I could hear the skipper and the navigator making final corrections for the run-in. We were late and, by the look of the city below, one of the last to arrive. The sky over the target was thick with flak and smoke, while at ground level dozens of individual fires and explosions were evident. Just as we started the straight and steady bomb run, a shadow blacked out the sky immediately over my head and I looked up in fright, thinking it was another fighter, but it was a Lancaster veering sideways across us, its bomb bay doors wide open. Then just as it parted company, I saw a vivid explosion near

Below: **Taxi rank. Lancs of No 83 Squadron, led by R5620, OL-H, taxi out from dispersals at Scampton prior to take-off for Bremen on 25 June 1942 — the third of 'Butch' Harris's much-publicised '1,000-bomber' raids. Piloted by Plt Off Farrow, R5620 was fated not to return from this sortie.** *IWM*

its cockpit, and watched the whole of its starboard wing peel away, with long strings of fire following the wing down — presumably split oil or petrol piping. The Lanc flicked over into a crazy spin and fell away and, seconds later, disappeared in a huge ball of fire as it blew up. Our Lanc lurched upwards, partly from the release of our load but partly, I'm sure, from the blast of that exploding Lanc below us. The skipper now weaved his way off to port, climbing as hard as he could, to get away from the flak zone.

'Once clear he told the flight engineer to check fuel and then relieve me in the mid-upper turret. I felt a tap on my boots and climbed down to let him in, then got back to my set to start getting a fix. There was a fair-sized hole in the wall to the left of me and I could look out over the wing — presumably done by flak over the target. However, my radio was still working with no apparent damage. Once in the clear, the skipper checked each crew station, then asked about

the mid-upper AG's state. "He's had it, skipper" came the reply. The skipper made no comment. The nav gave him the latest course to steer. We plodded homeward for about half an hour, then Jerry found us again. The rear gunner suddenly yelled, "Ju88 behind us, skipper. 1,000 yards!"... "Watch the bastard and tell me when to weave"... "He's staying out there for now, Skip"... "Here he comes!.. Go port, Skip!"... I hung on tight as the kite bounced left and down, then up and right. I could hear the rear guns hammering — I assumed the engineer was firing too — and then there was a crash like the gates of doom closing shut. My radio set just disappeared in front of my eyes, smashed to bits as shells ripped it apart; taking half my left hand and glove with it. I felt nothing for the moment, but just sat there looking at what was left of my left hand — a thumb and rags where the fingers should be. It took time to realise I'd been hit — only seconds perhaps but it seemed like hours. I

couldn't believe it. Again, my next thought was a ridiculous one — I had lost my gold wedding ring with the fingers!

'My next move was part-instinctive, part-training; I fumbled for a field dressing to cover the remnants of my hand and stop the bleeding. I couldn't find the dressing at first, my brain wasn't functioning properly yet. Then I got it out and ripped it open with my other hand and teeth and started bandaging the hand. My next thought was for something to tourniquet my left arm otherwise I'd bleed to death (I propably wouldn't have bled to death but panic of sorts was creeping in). Now I began to feel pain in my arm. I reported my wound to the skipper, but he never answered; too busy I suppose. I then took my intercom lead and wrapped it tightly around my left arm just above the elbow and hung on to it. The arm soon went numb and the pain subsided for the moment. All this went on while the aircraft was bouncing around as the skipper followed his gunners'

orders for evasive action. Minutes later the Lanc resumed an even keel; the immediate danger had apparently passed. When everything steadied up again, I got off the floor and got the navigator to tie a proper tourniquet on my arm, using one of his pencils as a knot-stick temporarily.

'That last attack had caused a fair amount of damage generally, apart from my cubbyhole. Most of the engineer's panel was shot out, the astro-dome shattered, and even the skipper's side window had been blown out, leaving him with one hell of a cold wind roaring in his left ear. Checking round the crew again, he got no response from the rear gunner this time, so sent me back to find out if the AG was OK, I knocked on the turret doors, no response. Tried the dead-man's handle; jammed. Using the fire axe, I chopped open the doors. The gunner was hunched up over his central control column. I thought he was dead — his turret perspex was a shambles — so began to haul him out

Above: **LM326, Z-Zebra of No 207 Squadron snapped from another Lanc on 17 October 1943. Just two nights later it was shot down over Hanover.** *IWM*

as best I could with one good arm. He woke as I pulled him and screamed, "Leave me alone, damn you!" He'd been hit in the guts and my rough handling merely increased the awful pain. I tried to talk him into being taken out so that we could treat his wound, but he merely said, "Leave me be, Stan, I've had it. Leave me in peace, for Christ's sake". I disconnected his intercom, then plugged myself in and told the skipper of his condition. "How bad is he?" . . . "I don't know, but it looks bloody awful" . . . "OK, do your best but don't move him . . . it's not far to home now". So I stayed with the wounded gunner, though there was sweet Fanny Adams that I could do to help him. Maybe just being there with him was some sort of comfort to him . . . I'll never know.

'We finally reached England without further interference and, despite no flaps or brake pressure, the skipper made a smooth landing. As we touched at full pelt the under-cart gave up the ghost and we shot off the end of the runway on our belly. Within seconds (it seemed) the blood-wagon (ambulance) and other cars were on the spot. They took away the mid-upper's body, then

Above: They also served . . . Ground crew erks of No 57 Squadron, East Kirkby settle down to await the return of their charges. *H. B. Mackinnon DFC*

Right: View of Hamburg from 18,000ft on the night of 30 January 1943, with another Lancaster silhouetted against the fury of explosions and fires below. *IWM*

Above: Hamburg two years later when U-boat pens and oil refineries were attacked with 12,000lb and 22,000lb bombs on 9 April 1945. *IWM*

Left: Relief. Flg Off P. J. Richards, skipper of C-Charlie, is chaired by his crew at Metheringham on 23 March 1944, on safe return from Frankfurt. *IWM*

Above: ED433, KM-V of No 44 Squadron at its Waddington dispersal in early 1943. It was eventually lost over Germany on 4 October that year.
L. Pilgrim DFC

Right: De-brief. Sgts Skilton, Kethro, Short and Williams, with their skipper Flg Off L. Pilgrim (far right) of No 44 Squadron relax after another sortie.
L. Pilgrim DFC

Below right: Flg Off 'Pop' Benner, a No 44 Squadron navigator, receives a DFC from the hands of HM King George VI, 1944.
L. Pilgrim DFC

extricated the rear gunner. He too had died; his stomach looked as it he'd been torn into two parts. The medico then noticed the mess I was in and bundled me into his Ford Eight and whisked me off to the sick bay, where they tidied up what was left of my left hand and cleaned the kid's blood off my face and neck and helmet etc. I spent the next two days in the sick bay and was then sent on 10 day's sick leave. I'd lost all four fingers of my left hand and part of the palm, but otherwise was OK — I'd been lucky. If that shell burst had been a few inches lower it would have taken my head off.

'On leave I had nightmares at night, often waking up yelling; my poor wife couldn't understand it but bore my "tantrums" with great patience. I had dreams of Lancs exploding and flak streams getting nearer and nearer, yet never quite reaching me. It proved to be my last taste of operations for they shuffled me off to a staff instructor's job on a ground wireless school, and I stayed there until demob. The dreams gradually simmered down with time, but even today I never take a shower, only a bath — the feel of that gunner's blood dripping on my face still recurs. And I hate rain.'

Memories

D. C. Tritton, a flight engineer, was one of a crew skippered by Pilot Officer Ewens which joined No 49 Squadron at Fiskerton in late September 1943 to commence their first tour of operations. Joining the squadron at the same time was Wg Cdr A. A. Adams (later, Air Marshal, CB, DFC) as the latest unit commander. Tritton remained with No 49 until May 1944 before being 'rested' from ops, and in the following account recalls much of the background to his winter of ops with the squadron:

'That early autumn was a period of glorious weather and after our first operation — 7 October, to Stuttgart in Lanc ED999 "A" — we went on leave. Our second operation was to Kassel on 22 October, in JB305, "E", and I well remember the vivid colouring of the night's target. A number of chemical works were incendiarised and the resulting lurid flames of incredible hues had to be seen to be believed. It was a month before we flew our third op, to Berlin on 22 November, in DV166 "F".

'"A" Flight, to which we were attached, was commanded by Sqn Ldr G. A. Day, a Short Service officer who had previously operated in the Middle East. He was a short, dapper man who, at first acquaintance, seemed rather a martinet. Mature reflection leads me to think that he was interested in pursuing the war efficiently to its close, and in a correct "soldierly" manner at that. He was greatly respected and not disliked. He did not suffer fools. I well recall going to the stores for an electric waistcoat for myself at his behest. The storeman said that issues could not be made in the afternoon and that, for me, was that. On my return Sqn Ldr Day spotted that I was sans waistcoat and asked why. When told he said simply, "You will tell them that I said you will have one". Conveyance of this simple message in a mild manner had an electric (sorry!) effect on the

Below: **Take her away. Lanc DV238 of No 49 Squadron being tractored to its dispersal slot by a blonde WAAF driver. An ex-No 619 Squadron aircraft, it later served with No 44 Squadron and was lost over Berlin on the night 16/17 December 1943, along with Plt Off D. A. Rollin and his crew.** *IWM*

Above: **Flight Engineers of No 189 Squadron, 1945. Fourth from left, centre row is the B Flt commander, Sqn Ldr McCracken; while far right, centre row is D. C. Tritton.** *D. C. Tritton*

Below: **No 49 Squadron's Lancasters prepare to taxi out. EA-T was L7453, an aircraft with a chequered career; serving with No 97 Squadron as OF-X, then Nos 83, 49 and 44 Squadrons before being allotted to 1661 Con Unit, where it was wrecked on 1 May 1943.** *IWM*

storeman. I was carefully fitted out at top speed and ushered out most courteously. If Day said "Jump", everybody jumped... When his tour expired Sqn Ldr Day was replaced by Sqn Ldr Evans, an observer coming up for his second tour. My log book shows that Sqn Ldr Day was our Flight commander for less than half our tour, but I can still remember every facet of him, such was his personality. "B" Flight was commanded by Sqn Ldr "Dusty" Miller. I remember him as a most pleasing character and an efficient Flight commander. Both Flight commanders left the squadron with a DSO.

'Wg Cdr Adams completed 14 operations with No 49 Squadron, was awarded a DFC, and posted as a group captain. His place was eventually taken by one of the newer Flight Lieutenants named Botting. We seemed to live for a while with odd bods doing such executive jobs as time would allow. The station was commanded by Grp Capt Grindell DFC who was very definitely the Station Commander in the office and around the camp, but was rather inclined to "live it up" in the Mess. Wg Cdr Adams was a relatively staid man of dignified bearing, and we wondered whether the strain of commanding an operational squadron or sharing quarters with the group captain was the greater! The wing commander tended to be an introvert, but the group captain was a full-blooded extrovert.

'The chain of command had another link in it at this period. Subordinate to Groups were Bases, each commanded by an Air Com-

modore, and Scampton was one such, No 52 Base, with Fiskerton and Dunholme Lodge as its satellite airfields. During my period with No 49, Scampton was non-operational (though remaining HQ for No 52 Base) as it was "closed" for the laying of concrete runways. Dunholme Lodge housed Nos 44 and 619 Squadrons, and Fiskerton No 49; though conditions at Dunholme sometimes became chaotic because they were lumbered with No 49 as well whenever things went wrong at Fiskerton. Flying from Dunholme Lodge was rather a nuisance for all concerned. Three squadrons milling about before take-off was bad enough, but queueing in the stack for landing was even worse. Usually we were briefed and fed at Fiskerton, then transported in crew coaches to Dunholme. This posed a security problem as briefed crews were thus out in the "ordinary" world. Drivers were not allowed to let us out until we reached our destination. One morning on return, when we had no cigarettes between us, a driver insisted that we each have one of his, as he couldn't let us out to buy any. We were doubly grateful, as cigarettes were scarce then.

'During the period that I served with No 49 Squadron, discipline was maintained to a good standard for all ranks. The wild tales I have heard of consistent indiscipline in some squadrons didn't apply. Some types were below par in personal standards of dress and deportment but not many and those were

Above: Flg Off J. B. Burnside, a flight engineer on No 619 Squadron, photographed at his panel on 14 February 1944. *IWM*

Left: Bomb aimer. Flt Lt P. Walmsley of No 619 Squadron, February 1944, holding the 'tit' for releasing the load. He was later awarded a DFC. *IWM*

not very badly. I have seen vagabonds like the Pirates of Penzance in some squadrons, but never with us. Obviously, Cochrane's influence had some bearing on this, but I always had the feeling that our squadron (and station) were definitely among the top-liners. The crews were generally a happy crowd and I can remember some wonderful evenings in the Sergeants' Mess. Morale was generally good but sometimes spirits slumped a little during the bad times, although the moral fibre didn't seem to suffer unduly. Several crews joined the squadron at about the same time as us, and became tour-expired at about the same time. Our little block seemed charmed. Unhappily I cannot say the same for those who were there when we arrived or those who joined subsequently. During the winter of 1943-44 the Luftwaffe's night fighters became increasingly successful, and the technique of laying mammoth flare "lanes" along the tracks of homeward-bound bombers was developed. Speaking purely personally, I found that cold glare surrounding one when flying through such a lane was capable of instilling more dread than any other weapon or circumstance. One could, of course, observe other bombers picked out by fighters diving out of the upper darkness — very demoralising!

'Fiskerton's call-sign was "Passout", and No 49 Squadron's was "Bandlaw". On arrival overhead our call would be "Hello Passout. Bandlaw J-Jig". Complete R/T silence was maintained before ops, and take-offs were arranged by strict time-keeping and clearance by Aldis (lamp) from the caravan. I have known people to be waiting their turn for take-off and getting a "green" to turn on, only to be given a "red" before having a chance to take-off. Those already airborne would then be recalled by W/T.

'Our main force loads were usually one 4,000lb "Cookie"—the name "Blockbuster" for these thin-cased canister bombs was dreamed up by the Press and used by the public, but they were *always* known as "Cookies" by us. The balance of the permissible load was then made up by canisters of small (4lb) hexagonal-shaped incendiary bombs. Later, incendiaries were much larger (eg 30lb), painted red, and fitted with fins. These were loaded in clusters, in circular racks, as distinct from the long canisters (Small Bomb Containers, or SBCs) used for the 4lb incendiaries. Bombing up was sometimes a frightful scramble and air crews were pressed into service to load the canisters, open cases, etc. Additional labour was later provided by an influx of aircrew cadets ("White Flash boys") posted to squadrons pending training. Whether our particular lads ever got to operational flying I know not, but their spirit was wonderful. With recruiting posters and dreams of glamour behind them, they settled down to the back-breaking toil that was a bomber armourer's lot. They knew all about Lancasters that didn't come back and those

Below: Erks. The men of 9619 Servicing Echelon and No 619 Squadron's Electrical Section at RAF Strubby in January 1945, with 'Chiefy' — Flt Sgt Tucker, NCO in charge — in dust coat.
C. R. Street

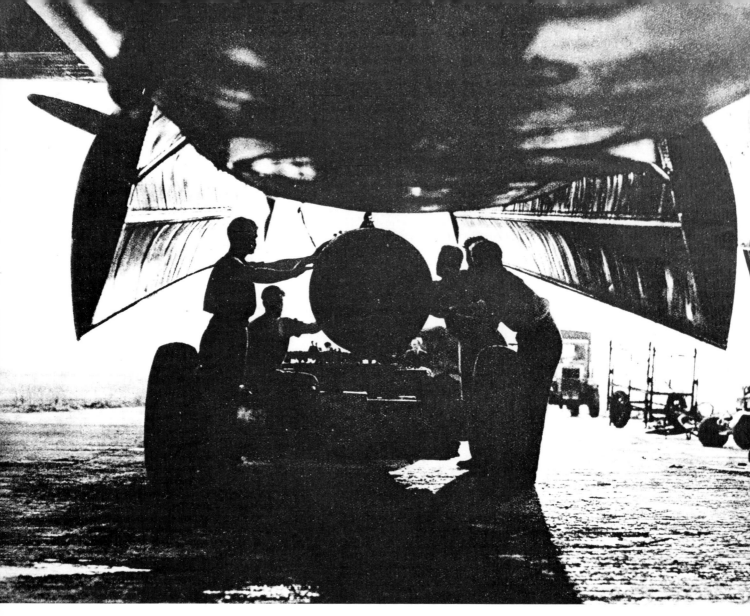

Above: Loading a 4,000lb HC 'Cookie' into the capacious Lanc bomb bay.

Right: Fire-load. SBC filled with 4lb incendiaries being rolled into position for loading.

that did with dead and wounded aboard. I asked one of our consistent young helpmates if he was still keen to fly, now that he knew what was involved. His eager face, shining eyes, and instant affirmative showed him to be completely undaunted, and I believe his little band were all like-minded.

'Occasionally we carried special 4,000lb bombs of the "Tallboy" type. These were similar to the 12,000 and 22,000lb bombs, but, of course, much smaller. They were machined all over, as distinct from the "as cast" condition of common HE. Their fins were precision aerofoils set with a slight helix which imparted a spinning motion. These were capable of very accurate aim. The fuses and pistols for these were different from those used in ordinary HE bombs, and some had long delay fuses which could be set up to 72 hours. Any attempt to remove such pistols would detonate the bomb; while if an armourer set one in cross-threaded the bomb was ruined and would go sky-high if unscrewed.

'Several Lancasters were written off during my tour with No 49 Squadron. A heavily-laden aircraft taking off with a degree of cross-wind would sometimes become unmanouevrable when airscrew torque built up. A laden Lancaster in full cry and hopelessly out of control was a petrifying sight. Occasionally sufficient control could be regained to effect some sort of take-off, and once airborne things sorted themselves out. One chap missed the control tower with inches to spare during one such take-off; he completed his operation, however. Usually the outcome was that the undercarriage would fail when skidding, and the aircraft would go down on one wing. Fire was inevitable and the pattern never varied — a glow of fire, hatches and doors bursting open, and seven, high-speed dots heading for the horizon! Nobody was killed in my time when involved in such spectacular episodes. I've known an aircraft burn to ashes without an explosion, but usually a shattering blast reduced the aeroplane to millions of fragments all over the aerodrome. The explosion would normally blow a hole in the runway large enough to submerge a house or two.

'One of the crews who joined the squadron with us was captained by Flying Officer Reg Hales. His rear gunner was a pleasant, tall Canadian Warrant Officer. This gunner was unfortunately brought back dead one night. He had been air-sick — anyone who has ridden a rear turret at night will understand — and, unknown to him, a particle of food had lodged in the oxygen valve of his mask. The atmospheric valve still functioned normally and he carried on with only thin air to breathe, not realising that anything was amiss. His life slipped away quietly between routine checks around the crew stations. We as a crew always took anoxia very seriously and made frequent intercom checks. Crew members moving about were expected to plug in at the first opportunity and report. However, not all crews were careful enough and one man wandered off with a portable (oxygen) bottle and no gloves. He was found unconscious in the rear fuselage and revived, but his hands had touched the aircraft structure, and he lost fingers from each hand due to frostbite.

Below: **En route. A No 189 Squadron Lanc, CA-D, sets out from Bardney, 1944.** *D. C. Tritton*

Above: Precision bombing of the Heligoland Bight on 18 April 1945 — a view from 19,000ft.

Right: Bird's-eye view of Cologne from 17,500ft on 2 March 1945

'Operational meals before ops were taken by all air crews in the Sergeants' Mess, whether commissioned or not. The target would set the mood of the crews; the Ruhr, long trips over occupied territory, and mining all produced laughing men, quick with a quip or leg pull. Reserved, silent men chewing without relish meant a long, hazardous haul. Morbidly, I sometimes reflected that for some it was usually the "last supper", but morbid thoughts were never framed into words. I think everyone must have had such thoughts at some time or other, but they were never spoken. It was an unwritten law that conversation must be cheerful, or one didn't converse. So strictly was it observed that not only was it unwritten, it was unmentionable.

'FIDO was completed, tested, and used operationally during our tour. A newspaper could be read with ease out of doors on a dark night when over a mile from FIDO. From the approach one seemed to be descending into the very jaws of Hell, and after touchdown the flames seemed to tower above. Fiskerton was the first station in 5 Group to be so fitted, and later Ludford Magna in 1 Group was similarly blessed. Our crew were involved in a non-operational incident with FIDO which did nothing to enhance our reputation as a crew, but we

were, unwittingly, responsible for the saving from total loss of another aircraft — and perhaps lives, had it fallen in the wrong place. During the afternoon of 1 December 1943 we were detailed to deliver Lancaster JB679, "D" to Swinderby. Just before taxying out we had a passenger wished upon us by Sqn Ldr Day with instructions to drop him at Wrexham in North Wales! We were ill-equipped for such a flight, but did not dare admit it to our Flight commander. All went well until a rapid deterioration of visibility coincided with gathering dusk. Swinderby refused us — I still think, unwisely — permission to land in view of the vis, although we were quite happy about it. We were ordered to proceed to Silloth in Cumberland. Being ill equipped for navigation, and having no great surplus of petrol, we refused the order and went to Fiskerton, asking for FIDO on arrival.

'FIDO duly came up and in we went, but to our amazement an Oxford followed us in right behind our tail! It transpired that it was the Station Flight's Oxford which had been away for the afternoon with two of the squadron's crew. On their return they saw that landing was out of the question (no radio was fitted — a common enough thing then) and as their petrol was nearly done were packing up preparatory to baling out. They couldn't believe their luck when they saw FIDO spring to life and stuck to us to get the benefit of it. I can still wince and raise a blush when I think of what the Flight commander said when he met us in the dispersal.

'On the night of 24 March 1944, bad visibility caused FIDO to be lit for the homeward-bound Lancs. While still over Holland we, in JB714, "J", could see the glow

and homed on it, maintaining an air plot and, later a GEE plot. Unknown to us somebody else was homing on it, presumably without air or GEE plots. We arrived over base and took our place in the stack, working steadily down until it was nearly our turn to land. We were listening out on R/T — we had VHF by then — and heard one of our Australian skippers say, "Funnel" and watched him turn in. To our horror we saw another Lanc turn in with him. A split second later the Aussie's voice called, "Jesus Christ, there's someone in the funnel with me!" "Overshoot" came the reply and we saw him pull away, while the other Lanc went in to pile up on our runway (no casualties). Fooled by long-range R/T, and not knowing that FIDO existed at stations other than Ludford Magna, he had been talking to Ludford and circling Fiskerton. We were immediately diverted to Waddington where we just scurried in before a complete clamp there. The BBC Recording Unit was at Fiskerton that night and subsequently broadcast our night's operations.

'Two crews were involved in unusual operational incidents over Denmark, at different times. Flying Officer "Jock" Simpson was outward bound one night when he and his crew were startled by a tremendous crash from beneath their feet. Their first thoughts were that a bomb had exploded and the load was hastily jettisoned. Immense vibration shook the aircraft and this was traced to the starboard inner engine. Feathering produced an instant cure, but it was obvious that many services and instruments were not working. Jock flew home with no gyro flying instruments, in pitch darkness. Inspection after landing showed that an airscrew blade had suffered fatigue

Above: Ground crew dispersal huts were occasionally minor works of 'art'; exemplified here by the crew of Lanc PA187, 'O-Orange' of No 467 Squadron RAAF in April 1945. Seated centre is Flg Off W. K. Boxsell DFC, the skipper of 'Orange' then. *V. Auborg*

and eighteen inches of tip had ripped into the bomb bay. Jock Simpson and his crew survived their tour and (I believe) the war.

'The other incident involved Flight Lieutenant Bill Heeley and his crew. Bill was a Canadian, with a loud voice and laugh. He too was outward bound when he felt a jar through the aircraft. Looking out along the port main plane he saw a Ju88 sitting on his wing tip, with the shadowy shape of the pilot visible. The impression lasted only a fraction of a second before the Junkers fell away, taking ten feet or so of the Lanc's wing with it. Bill managed to retain control, while the crew saw the Ju88 burst into flames on impact with the ground. Bill's port engine was pushed askew and the airscrew bent beyond redemption. He limped home on three with a short port wing and was awarded a DFC. Shortly afterwards Bill and his crew were detached to "experimental duties" at Newmarket. Whilst flying in company with the fighter with which they had been "affiliating", Bill's dinghy burst out of its stowage (upper skin of starboard wing) and the Lanc went in straight from low level — all were killed.

'No 49 Squadron's aircraft, during my period with them, carried none of the painted mascots, symbols or cartoons that decorated the sides of so many bombers. Past experience had caused a superstition that such things were unlucky. A newcomer pilot officer wanted his aircraft embellished with a white rabbit. The ground crew refused to do it, or even help him to rig trestles to do it himself. Nothing daunted, he completed the job single-handed. Shortly afterwards he was missing from ops in that same Lanc. Nobody repeated the experiment during our tour, and

when I saw 49 again in 1945 the aircraft were still plain.

'For the greater part of our tour we were issued with tins of California orange juice as part of our flying ration. This was a priceless nectar. It cleaned the palate and one felt new again. Then from the Air Ministry came the decision that two oranges would be more nourishing and that became the issue instead. This was absurd. Even the least vigilant types were loth to take time off to meddle with an orange. They made an intolerable mess of a navigator's chart, and were a nuisance to a wireless operator. A gunner couldn't use them at all as they were too big to carry in their clothing, and froze hard as steel if left in the turret. Handing a warm, soft orange in to a gunner was of little help to him; he couldn't peel it with his gloves on, and daren't take them off. The Air Ministry dieticians concerned must have suffered incandescent ears for the rest of the war!

'The work of the ground crews cannot possibly go unmentioned. Aircraft were only taken into a hangar for major repairs or for routine inspections. This meant many hours' work at all sorts of queer times in all weathers. Come hail, thunder or snow, the crews slaved to keep the aircraft adjusted, repaired and cleaned. They cursed and grumbled, as troops have always done, but their inner sense of duty was high. Aircraft returning damaged from ops were frequently patched and re-engined by breakfast time, regardless of weather. I believe our establishment was for 24 aircraft, though in practice we owned between 17 and 23 at any one time. I cannot recall more than one aircraft ever being unavailable (for ops) due to unserviceability.'

Return Trip

In the months preceding the Allied invasion of Normandy in June 1944, Bomber Command generally concentrated on the destruction of the French rail and road communications systems south and east of the proposed landing beaches. One such target was Tours, and among the many crews despatched by 5 Group against this target on the night of 7 May was that of Lancaster BIII, JB723, 'L' of No 57 Squadron, based at East Kirkby. Skippered by Ron Walker, a Sussex man, the crew was the 'usual' mixture of men from widely varying locations and nationalities, including two Canadians, a Welshman, and others from Dorset, Oxford and Hampshire. Having crewed up at 16 OTU, Upper Heyford in mid-1943, the crew underwent 'heavy conversion' training at 1660 HCU, on Stirlings, then completed the Lancaster flying school course, and finally reported to No 57 Squadron at East Kirkby on 17 March 1944. Just four nights later Walker's crew flew their first operational sortie together — Berlin, a seven and a half hours' trip. The trip to Tours on 7/8 May

1944 became their 14th 'op'. A few days later Bertram Mackinnon — 'Mac' — the navigator, jotted down his own account of the sortie:

'With a bomb load comprised of one 4,000lb "Cookie" and 16 500lb MC bombs, we had been briefed to attack Tours in bright moonlight. Take-off from East Kirkby was at 0038hrs, but the story really begins as we were running up to the target at 8,000 feet. We were a little early and were orbiting when the Controller informed us that the markers were "bang-on" and we could bomb. So round we turned and Ken Bly, the bomb aimer, took over. The first intimation of really serious opposition came when Ken reported horizontal tracer on the starboard side, and Bill Carver, the rear gunner, a fighter attacking someone on the port quarter. Bill was watching him carefully, and Tom Quayle, the mid-upper gunner, as usual, was searching the heavens above, with a crafty eye on the starboard. Ken gave a series of "Left-left-left-left", and then the always welcome "Bombs gone" — followed by that "gluck-gluck" of the bombs falling off. (The first time I heard them I thought the bottom was falling off the 'plane...)

'Things happened quickly then. Tom yelled, "Fighter, fighter, corkscrew port — GO!" and Ron needed no second telling. We went with a vengeance, the bombs spraying off in all directions. We at the front heard something firing and the ominous thuds of someone hitting us; where we didn't know. Just as we were pulling out of the initial dive we heard the rear gunner yelling, "Are you all right in front skipper?" — and we hastened to reassure him. In the meantime Tom had seen this fighter about 400 yards astern just above us and identified it, thank God, in a split second as a Ju88, and opened fire simultaneously with the Ju88. In his own words, "The nose of the blighter was like one ball of fire"; while another peculiarity was that its engines were encircled by two pale blue haloes of flame — surely the "Devil's Diadems". We were doing some 250mph in that first dive, yet the Ju88 passed us in a vertical dive. We prayed that that dive terminated on the ground and not before.

Left: **K. E. Bly DFC, RCAF (Bomb aimer), Roland Hammersley DFM (W/Op), H. B. Mackinnon DFC (Nav).**

Above: **W. Carver (rear AG, left) and T. Quayle (MU/AG)**

Above right: **Ron Walker (pilot) and E. Chung (engineer)**

Right: **Warrant Officer A. F. 'Red' Browne DFM (air gunner). All were the No 57 Squadron crew of Ron Walker, East Kirkby.**
H. B. Mackinnon DFC

'We continued to corkscrew, completing two cycles. Ken yelled to the skipper to keep weaving, but he decided, perhaps wisely, to turn on to course 323 True. We were deep enough into France without going any deeper. We had turned on to course and were clear of the defences when suddenly — and only then — did Bill pipe up again with, "Skipper, I've had it". Ginger Hammersley, the W/Op/AG, immediately ran back to the rear turret, plugged in his intercom and told Bill he was there. Bill was in a sad state. Face, arms and legs were simply streaming with blood. Helped by Ginger, he managed to get out of his turret and, in spite of the fact that the aircraft was swaying rather badly, got on to the rest bed. In the front Ken had thoughtfully clipped his 'chute on, ready to exit with some speed, but hearing the news about Bill he came back, first to help Ginger and then to take over the turret. He soon realised the futility of doing the latter. It was just a jumbled mess of bullet-pocked metal with merely a few jagged pieces of perspex left. It would not rotate and the hand rotation

81

gear had been hit and made useless by flak. So Ken returned to help dress Bill's wounds.

'In the meantime Esmond Chung, the flight engineer, had checked the engines and discovered that the port outer had no oil pressure and had to be feathered at once. This destroyed any possibility of using the rear turret, and the GEE box was also out of action. To counterbalance the loss of an engine Ron began to wind the rudder trim, only to find that this just went round and round and did little more. So he had to jam the rudder hard over to starboard. Esmond went down to the nose and hung on to the rudder bar to ease the strain off Ron a bit. The obvious thing to do was to get some rope and tie the rudder bar, and Ginger was asked to do this but was too busy. Ken and Ginger had got Bill on to the rest bed and were cutting away all clothing around his legs. They revealed several nasty wounds which were bleeding profusely, in both legs. Ransacking every available first aid outfit, they began to swathe him up and put a tourniquet on each leg. It was tricky work. They daren't have much light about because we rather desired to hide our light under a very big bushel. His legs finished, they then

started on Bill's face which was also badly cut about. Ken first of all slapped a field dressing on, but Ginger mildly pointed out that Bill would find it a little difficult to breathe through a hulking great wad of cotton wool. So Ken reversed it so that Bill might be able to breathe, but could hardly talk. Eventually the matter was righted and Bill lay there swathed on legs, arms and face, looking more like Tutankhaman than any man I'd ever seen. Ken told Ginger to get some water, and without hesitation he broke open the dinghy pack and opened a can of water which Bill sucked all the way back.

'With our rear defenceless, it was obviously best to get right down on the deck, which Ron did. We literally had to go up to get over trees and, on one occasion, Ron with eyesight as marvellous as ever flew *round* a church steeple which loomed right in our

path. Under the moon it was almost as bright as day and we roared over field, farm and village; the three engines giving us some 180mph. I don't recommend as a general habit flying a big bomber at nought feet with one engine gone and the rudder trimming finished, but Ron did it. The long-wanted rope was finally forthcoming and tied around the rudder bar. This gave Esmond the chance to get a real leverage on it and took quite a lot of strain off Ron's leg. Meanwhile I announced that we were only 50 miles from the French coast. We'd been warned we might have a hot reception there from flak, so it was obviously necessary to abandon our hedge-hopping and we pulled up to 10,000 feet. We crossed the French coast nicely on

track and set course to miss going over any of the Channel Islands, the occupants of which were still hostile and likely to shoot at us.

'Bill seemed to have alternate periods of semi-consciousness and brightness. We kept him off the intercom as long as possible. It is difficult to discuss the condition of anyone while they can listen, but eventually he insisted on being plugged in. It was very clear that we had to get him to a hospital as soon as possible. Once clear of the Channel Islands we set course over the 80-odd miles to the nearest aerodrome. We'd been flying about three minutes on this last leg when Tom reported an unidentified 'plane which was dogging us astern. "Is it a Lancaster?"... "Just a minute" said Tom, "No... it's a fighter. Turn starboard a bit, skipper". We heard a burst of machine gun fire and then began to corkscrew. Tom had

Below: Lanc B1, RA530 of No 57 Squadron, which was destroyed in a take-off crash in Stockney village on 20 March 1943 when setting out against Bohlen.

got a really long burst at the Jerry, who did not appreciate it and dived away to port. Whoever he was he hadn't much pluck, thank goodness, for we were pretty easy meat then. However, we saw him no more.

'After long last the most welcome coast came up, we passed over it at St Alban's Head, and began to send a MAY-DAY call over the R/T. Hurn answered us faintly and didn't light up. Another 'drome — Tarrant Rushton — ahead was lit up and we went in there. We had the pleasure of hearing other kites being ordered to circle while we landed. Ron ordered the ambulance over the R/T and made a good landing; still, he always could land better on three than four engines...! Once down, Ron brusquely asked where the ambulance was; it was right behind us and Bill, largely by his own efforts but helped by willing hands, was soon away to the station sick quarters. Six extremely thankful men followed him out of the machine. Transport was waiting for us. First we had to be de-briefed, and then had a more-than-welcome breakfast. We were all worried about Bill and went round to the sick quarters. We nearly hit the MO on the way, and heard the glad news that while Bill had lost a lot of blood, his injuries were not too serious. Shrapnel had hit his legs, arms, while shattered perspex had caused most of the damage to his face. Now he was safely away in Shaftesbury Hospital to receive the attention that a very gallant man deserved. We all wondered at his fortitude and courage in somehat harrowing circumstances. He was literally "bloody but unbowed". Our pilot, Ron Walker, was deservedly given the DFC, but Bill Carver, most undeservedly, was given nothing.'

Above: Angel. WAAF wireless operator guiding a returning Lanc back to 'roost' at Scampton, February 1943. *IWM*

Right: A No 57 Squadron Lancaster over Scampton, April 1944. *IWM*

84

Above left: Yank in a Lanc. Lt Jack Russell USAAF, skipper of Lancaster ED655, DC-X, of No 57 Squadron, June 1943. *J. Lazenby DFC*

Above: Flt Lt T. B. 'King' Cole DFC (4th from right) and his Lanc R5691, VN-K of No 50 Squadron. With a different crew this aircraft was lost over Milan on 4 October 1942. *T. B. Cole DFC*

Left: Return from Berchtesgaden. Wg Cdr David Balme DSO, DFC (2nd from right, standing) and his No 227 Squadron crew at Strubby on 27 April 1945, with his 'gaggle leader' — marked Lanc PA280, 9J-P, in background. *D. S. Richardson DFC*

An Air Gunner Remembers

Ron Winton was trained as a Wireless Operator/Air Gunner and eventually joined No 207 Squadron at Spilsby, Lincolnshire on 20 July 1944 to commence his first operational tour. His crew were Flt Lt John White (the ex-Manchester speedway rider 'Jack' White) as captain, Sgt Aubrey Wykes (bomb aimer), Sgt Bob Webb (flight engineer), Sgt Ted Peek (navigator), Flg Off Lloyd Hahn (a Canadian mid-upper gunner), and Sgt Albert Tweddle (rear gunner). He recalls:

'We commenced our tour on 31 July 1944 with a daylight raid on a V1 storage depot at Rilley-la-Montagne, France. We were as green as grass and because of a mix-up over which aiming point we should have been on, we found ourselves over the target alone and

the ground gunners gave us all they had. We came back full of holes including a punctured tail wheel, which gave Albert a rough ride when we landed. However, we lived to tell the tale — and never made the same mistake again! We then did an assortment of both day and night raids for the next few weeks before going on our first leave.

'The next "shaky do" was on our 13th trip on 12/13 September — and with all those "13s" we knew we had to have some incident. The target was the Volkswagen factory at Stuttgart, bombing height was 17,750 feet, bomb load was one 4,000lb Cookie and 14 J-Type Clusters, and the flying time was seven hours. Our Lancaster was PD217, EM-Z, which our crew had been allocated and in which we flew most of our

Below: **Navs union meeting. Navigators of No 227 Squadron at Strubby, April 1945. Second row, centre, is the Nav Leader, Flt Lt E. Kirby DFM.** *D. S. Richardson DFC*

Above: Flt Lt John White's
No 207 Squadron crew in front of
Lancaster PB293, EM-W.
R. Winton

Left: Lloyd Hahn (in turret), Ted
Peek and Ron Winton, No 207
Squadron, in late 1944. *R. Winton*

Above: Save me from my friends. Port wing damage to EM-Z, PD217 of No 207 Squadron after an air collision with a No 57 Squadron Lanc over Stuttgart on the night of 12/13 September 1944 — John White's crew's 13th operational sortie. *R. Winton*

Right: 'Tammy' Simpson, rear gunner to Mick Martin of No 617 Squadron, at Blida airfield on 25 July 1943, cheerfully displaying the damage to his turret vision panels. *W. Howarth*

operations. The first thing to go wrong was Lloyd Hahn was unable to fly due to a severe head cold. This rather upset Lloyd and we weren't very happy about it either because it meant taking a gunner from another crew. He was Flying Officer Gutheridge and, of course, there was nothing wrong with him; it was just that crews didn't like such changes. It was a fairly normal trip up to the target area when, just as we were approaching the target, I was (as normal) off the intercom, my call light started flashing like mad, and Ted Peek shouted to me, "The intercom has gone!" All hell then broke out.

'I wrote a hurried note to pass up front to tell John to switch on the TR1196 which was normally used for Air-Ground R/T comms but also had an emergency intercom facility. The note never reached John and in fact was never seen again. After a few seconds of checking, I decided that the Low Tension Accumulator must have run out, so it meant a switch to the spare acc. At that time the two accs were positioned under the navigator's table, right over against the port side — a worse place couldn't have been found anywhere. To get to them between the navigator's bench seat and the table with flying gear on was an impossibility so I had to strip off my flying helmet (no oxygen at

17,750 feet . . .), parachute harness and Mae West, then dive under the table. Fortunately, my guess was right, and the intercom came back on as the target came in to the bombsight. I came out from under the table panting for breath. We went through the target and then started to settle down when suddenly I felt the aircraft start a pretty severe corkscrew.

'The next thing I remember was a violent shudder as though the aircraft had stopped and then shot forward again. I went forward and my head hit the transmitter, and then I was back in my seat again just as suddenly. A quick look at Ted was enough to tell me something had happened but we were still flying. I switched to intercom and was surprised to find there was complete silence. We had ceased to corkscrew and things seemed normal again, so I decided to ask later what it was all about. What had happened in fact was that a fighter had attacked us, and during the corkscrew we had come up under another Lanc. John must have had his eyes on the blind flying panel — as was normal in a corkscrew — and didn't see it. Wykie, the bomb aimer, was the only one who saw the other Lanc looming up; he shouted "DIVE!" and, luckily, John's reaction was instantaneous, though he couldn't avoid a collision and we struck the other Lanc in its bomb bay with our port wing-tip. There was no doubt in our minds that Wykie's shout and John's instinctive reaction had saved both our and the other crew's lives.

'John flew "Zebra" back with the control column almost fully over to starboard due to the damage to our port aileron. When we had got well out of enemy range I climbed into the astro-dome and shone the Aldis lamp on to the wing-tip. Gutheridge in the mid-upper turret said he couldn't see any wing-tip. Arriving back over base we couldn't contact Airfield Control because our fixed aerials had been severed. We got a green from the caravan after I'd flashed a "Z" at it. John made a perfect landing and Op No 13 was over. Incidentally, shortly after that all the Lancs on the squadron had the accumulators mentioned moved to a new location just behind the main spar where they could be reached easily. There was an inquiry into the incident and the entries in the nav's logs, with times and positions of the collision, coincided perfectly; we had clobbered a No 57 Squadron Lanc from East Kirkby, our Base HQ and close neighbour. "Zebra" got a new port wing outer section and we were back on ops in her on 19 September. Target that night was München Gladbach and this was the op on which Wg Cdr Guy Gibson VC was acting as Master Bomber and was killed. We heard him quite clearly on the VHF telling the lads to "beat it for home",

Below: **Flt Lt J. A. Howard DFC of No 619 Squadron, February 1944.** *IWM*

Left: WO K. Draycott (left) and Flt Sgt D. Ringham, both air gunners in John Chatterton's No 44 Squadron Lancaster crew for Z–Zebra, 1945. *J. Chatterton DFC*

Right: Arthur Haywood in his mid-upper 'office' of Lancaster PA280, 9J-P of No 227 Squadron, from Strubby, during a trip over Dusseldorf to view bomb damage, 1 June 1945. *D. Richardson DFC*

Below: Turtle-back. Rear gunner in a Lancaster with 'folding' armour-plate protection in the turret centre panel.

but nothing further was heard from him — a great loss to the RAF, especially 5 Group.

'Squadron life at that period was a bit hectic and short-lived by a good percentage of crew members. I thoroughly enjoyed it myself; I was single unlike most of the other members of my crew, and although I was looking forward to finishing a tour I was most anxious not to lose the comradeship of squadron life. It is quite true what most aircrew would say; that at the beginning of the tour one expected to get shot down, but as the tour went on and the crew became more experienced they also became more relaxed. Then towards the end, when there were only a few more trips to do, a crew became tense and each op was like starting all over again. Certainly, my crew was no exception. The NCO members of our crew spent our leisure hours at the pub in Thorpe St Peter, then known as the Queen Victoria but now known as the The Huntsman; and of course dear old Skegness — "Skeggie" — was a real favourite.

'I must mention a certain Australian skipper, one Flg Off Loveless, who very nearly did a good job of destroying RAF Spilsby while taking off on his first op on 1 November. He apparently hadn't heeded the warnings of what a fully-loaded Lanc would do under full power and, of course, the inevitable happened. He started off down the runway and we watched it start to swing, which got worse and worse until the Lanc swung right off the runway and made a bee-line for the control tower. Luckily for the control tower three Halifaxes had been diverted to Spilsby the night previous and it

was these which took the full force of the collision. There was immediate fire but the whole crew got out without a scratch. It wasn't long before the bombs started to go off and that put paid to the rest of the squadron getting off airborne, us included. Bomb splinters were flying all over the place and we beat a hasty retreat behind a hay stack, where we were joined by some local farmers. By this time two of the Hallies and the Lanc were burning, but one Halifax was untouched. A flight engineer of one of the diverted crews jumped into this Halifax and was starting it up to taxy it out of the danger area when the nose swung round as more bombs exploded. The nose of the Halifax was blown off completely, and the poor fellow, a Canadian, was badly injured and died later. He was the only casualty. Many buildings were badly damaged and the runways were

Above: Flg Off Graham H. Farrow RAAF and his No 463 Squadron crew at Waddington. *L. Cottroll*

Right: Crew of Lancaster ED611, JO-U of No 463 Squadron RAAF at Waddington. From left: Rod Brownlee (nav); Kevin Brett (B/A); Milton 'Pete' Wickes (pilot); Lou Botting (engineer); Fred Boddy (MU/AG); while kneeling are L. Cottroll (rear/AG) and Bob Jenkins (W/Op). *L. Cottroll*

Below right: Lanc RF141, 'Uncle Joe Again' of No 463 Squadron RAAF, Waddington, which was usually skippered by Flg Off 'Pete' Wickes DFC, RAAF. *L. Cottroll*

covered in bomb splinters. All air crews who hadn't got away, along with anybody else who could be spared, had to sweep the runways clear for the returning aircraft, which, naturally, we didn't mind doing. Loveless was to write-off a further two Lancs before finishing his tour and leaving the squadron — we all said he must have had a charmed life!

'We completed 27 operations. Our last trip on 18 December was to Gdynia to attack the battleship *Lützow* and the docks. We were not on the original crew listing but because another crew chap had not returned from leave we had to take their place — fate? Two aircraft from each of the squadrons on the raid were detailed to bomb the ship which was unmarked by TIs as a surprise element. My crew and another experienced crew captained by Flt Lt Buchanan, a New Zealander, were the No 207 Squadron pair, and we were both shot down by night fighters over the target. We were in LM671, EM-S, and lost both our starboard engines plus other damage and had to ditch in the Baltic. Flt Lt Buchanan and his crew in NG144, EM-G, were all lost in the attack. We were picked up by the German air-sea rescue nine hours later, very cold and wet, and were PoWs for the rest of the war. Lloyd Hahn, the mid-upper gunner, was wounded in the attack and as a result had to have the lower part of his right arm amputated, and was later repatriated back to Canada. I had been commissioned only a few days before our last trip, so myself and John White went to Stalag Luft 1 at Barth, on the Baltic coast; while the NCO crew members all went to a camp in Poland. We were all released by the Russians after the war had ended.'

Below: Veteran. R5868, PO-S ('Sugar') of No 467 Squadron, Waddington with some of its ground crews, 1944. On ground, right, is Flt Sgt Cyril Henshaw, NCO in charge of maintenance. S-Sugar is now on permanent display in the RAF Museum at Hendon.

Kaleidoscope

After nearly 40 years memories inevitably grow hazy, particularly about events and incidents which occurred in the heat of action when youthful minds and young blood ran fast, and near-brushes with death were almost a common experience. Yet certain incidents remain crystal clear, permanently fixed on the screen of recollection, no matter how long ago these happened; recalled perhaps by some brief annotation in a faded log book, a crumpled snapshot, or the passing sight of a mouldering control tower in an empty field. Maybe from a chance query at a squadron reunion. 'Ever know what happened to Tommy L............, my skipper?' ... 'Yeah, got the chop at an FTS when some sprog sliced off the tail of his kite' ... Poor little Tommy ... just 19 years old, yet he'd brought us back from Hamburg on two engines and half a tail ... they gave him a DFM for that show, too ... they didn't know he'd been as sick as a cow when the reaction set in later that evening ...

Fred Jones was a bomb aimer who crewed up at Upper Heyford with Peter Anderson RCAF (skipper), Glynn Williams (Nav), Sgt Swetman (flight engineer), Flg Off Lush W/Op), and two gunners Sgt Channon (MU/AG) and Flg Off Trilsbeck RCAF (rear AG). After a Lancaster conversion course at Coningsby, the crew reported to No 97 Squadron at Woodhall Spa, and flew their first operation on 5 October 1942, to Aachen in Lancaster R5490. Here Fred Jones recalls a few operations from that first tour — which was, in his words, 'Not too much trouble — 30 take-offs and 30 completed':
'Prior to our first op we'd had the usual cross-country exercises but little experience of crossing the coast line. After take-off we climbed on course. When we reached the English Channel we were above cloud and searchlights were fingering the sky. We couldn't see the coast line but the cloud thinned ahead of us and flak began to burst around us. Our skipper decided it was our

Below: Whatever the weather. Lancasters of No 463 Squadron RAAF at Waddington on 1 March 1944. The unit had only recently been formed — on 25 November 1943 — from a nucleus of C Flight, No 467 Squadron RAAF.

Far right, top: Belly-full. Lancaster bomb load lined up prior to being 'digested' in the bomb bay.

Far right, bottom: Seeing 'em off. Erks — male and female — wave off a Lancaster bound for Berlin, June 1944.

own anti-aircraft guns firing on us so he ordered the W/Op to fire the colours of the day. The W/Op obeyed the order and pressed the trigger of the signal pistol, which was ready loaded and fixed into the roof. The cartridges exploded and the colours of the day floated down. We then saw that the flak was coming from the enemy coast up ahead. Almost immediately after we fired, nearly every other aircraft in the vicinity fired their Very pistols and the air was full of Very lights. This evidently puzzled the Germans as they ceased fire and doused the searchlights!

'6 November 1942. We flew in Lanc R5917 to Genoa with a 900×4lb incendiary load and attacked the target in clear weather and turned for home. The cloud above and below us prevented us from getting a fix, and GEE was only just coming into general use. The navigator used the Met-forecast winds and I was in the nose as we neared what we thought was our base. I saw a piece of coast line through a small break in the low cloud and reported it to the captain. The navigator thought it must be the Wash, a familar landmark. The captain asked for a course to Woodhall Spa but before he got it a WAAF's voice called, "Hello Nemo, hello Nemo". The skipper answered with "Hello Darky" and the WAAF then asked if we needed any help. Our captain, having confidence in his crew,

replied "No thanks", then just as an afterthought asked, "Where are we?". The reply shook us. "You are over Exeter". After a moment's stunned silence the captain politely requested help. We were instructed to watch for rockets breaking through the low cloud and to circle them as we descended. We did just that and landed safely. There wasn't enough gas left in the tanks to measure. The forecast winds had given way to opposing winds, and but for that alert WAAF we would have landed in the drink. We didn't thank the WAAF personally but we often wondered who she was.

'17 November 1942. Our seventh operation, and we went to Danzig to lay three mines. This type of mine would explode if dropped from higher than 1,000 feet, and it was not as well packed as the later types, which could be laid from up to 15,000 feet. We flew to Karlskrona on the Swedish coast — it was a novelty to see all the lights on — and the Swedes fired some flak, but it was generally away from us. We descended to 600 feet to lay the mines and flew over Danzig. We had been told at briefing that the anti-aircraft gunners were more of a "home guard" than the regular troops, and our experience seemed to bear this out. Turning north over the city we commenced to sow

Left: Damage at Politz, a priority target in 1943-45.

Below: St Cyr airfield after being effectively put out of action by 'smother-bombing'.

ST CYR A/F and P.
Signal Equipment Sta
K 2774

mines in between the mainland and the outer spit of land. As the first mine dropped searchlights were turned on and they started firing at us. They promptly stopped firing and extinguished the lights when we returned their fire.

'*17 December 1942*. Our eleventh op was briefed as an "alarm and despondency" raid. The date was 17 December, and our aircraft R5538. The normal raids on Germany had been curtailed because of the poor weather, and this idea was for a small force of bombers to spread out over Germany and bomb separate targets. Our nominal target was a small town named Neustadt. We flew at low level and as we crossed the Dutch coast the mid-upper gunner informed the captain that his turret was frozen. The skipper decided to try the bomb doors, as it would be useless to carry on if the bomb doors were frozen or the hydraulics were u/s. The bomb doors opened OK but they wouldn't close again. However, the skipper decided to carry on with the bomb load of two 1,000lb HE and 88 30lb incendiary bombs exposed. We climbed to a bombing height of 4,000 feet when the navigator told us we were near the target. I'd been map-reading and I thought we were over some placed called Diepholtz, but the skipper decided to bomb and we circled while I searched for a target. All was quiet until the

Above: **Happy crew after returning from Stuttgart in Lanc R-Robert, 14/15 April 1943.**

first bomb exploded, after which we got a hot reception — they'd been hoping we'd go away. Judging by the amount of flak it was a well-defended target, but we never did find out the name of the place. This was the last "alarm and despondency" raid — for Lancasters anyway — because the night's losses showed that the "alarm and despondency" was not all on the enemy side.

'28 December 1942. Our own aircraft, H-Harry, being u/s, we were detailed to take A-Apple (R5548) on operations. This aircraft was usually flown by Sqn Ldr "Darky" Hallows. We took A-Apple for an air test in the morning and were briefed for a raid later that night. It was growing dusk when we went out to dispersal, but before we could get aboard the operation was scrubbed and we piled back into the truck. Just as we reached the control tower we heard a dull boom. A-Apple had been broken in two by its own photo-flash. The armourer was killed and two other ground staff were injured.

'8 January 1943. Lanc ED310. A small force bombed Essen using the Wanganui technique, sky markers laid by Mosquitos using Oboe. We found Essen covered in cloud. The photos showed no ground detail so we tried again next night.

'9 January 1943. Lanc R5896. A small force of about 20 aircraft bombed the sky markers. It was cloudy again but we brought back a photo with ground detail not far from Krupps.

'2 February 1943. Lanc W4249. Our worst trip. We had just released our bomb load over Cologne and closed the bomb doors when we were coned by searchlights. The skipper lost no time in putting the nose down in a steep dive. I was still down with the bombsight. Empty cartridge cases were floating around in the air, and specks of dust looked like gold dust. The flight engineer's tool bag was literally "hanging up" — the handle was at the bottom. We soon lost the searchlights and the pilot was striving to get us out of the dive. Vigorous use of the trimming wheel on the right-hand side of his seat finally got us out of it, only to have the aircraft try to stand on its tail. I was jammed against the floor by inertia and made several futile attempts to get my parachute out of its stowage. As the aircraft rose steeply all four engines quit and we were left in what seemed to be complete

silence. Another correction by the pilot and we were on a more even keel, then the engines came back to life with a very comforting roar. We set course for base and were about halfway home when the mid-upper gunner reported that the photo-flash had not gone with the bombs but was in fact on the floor inside the aircraft. We all thought of the fate of A-Apple on 28 December, and after examining it and reporting to the skipper, it was decided to let sleeping photo-flashes lie. It was a *very* relieved crew that landed back safely that morning. A small projection was added to the top of the flare chute to prevent a recurrence of this incident.

'*13 February 1943*. Lorient. Lanc W4249. The object of the raid was to destroy the housing and other facilities. Our HC bombs had little effect on the U-boat pens. The Pathfinders were to mark the target with ground markers, but when we arrived at the target I could see the markers were off to one side. The skipper told me to bomb the target if I could see it. I bombed the target and when we were de-briefed the Intelligence officer thought it would have been wiser to have bombed the markers. However, we obtained an aiming point photograph, and got an aiming point "token" signed by the AOC, AVM, W. A. Coryton.

'*16 February 1943*. Lanc ED591. Lorient again. Over the target we were faced with a similar situation as on the previous raid. The skipper thought twice before telling me to bomb what I could see. We were very happy to find we had another AP photo, and this time the "token" was signed by the new AOC, R. A. Cochrane. The pilot's private "Good show" meant a lot to me.

'Our pilot finished his tour but the crew still had two ops to do, and I finished my last two with Flt Lt Les Munro (of later Dambuster fame). It was to be December 1944 before I was back on operations, this time with No 44 Squadron at Spilsby. I finished with another eight operations with Sqn Ldr Ferguson as my pilot. I found very many changes — H2S, Loran, GEE, were in all aircraft and with a greater range, bantam cameras to take pictures of the GEE screen. The biggest change was the VHF, which enabled us to call up base at a much greater range enabling us to get back to base every time — and on time too.'

Ambush at Nuremberg

In terms of casualties alone, the bombing operations undertaken against the city of Nuremberg on the night of 30 March 1944 proved to be the most disastrous ever sustained by Bomber Command throughout the air war. It is true that higher numerical losses in aircraft had already occurred in RAF operations eg the air battles over Dieppe in 1942; while in terms of percentages of a bomber force despatched upon particular occasions, the most tragic of the war were without question those of the Fairey Battle squadrons in France during the last three weeks of May 1940. Nevertheless, the toll of the bomber force sent to Nuremberg on that fateful night became a byword for disaster among the ranks of Bomber Command thereafter. A total of 1,009 aircraft were involved in all forms of operations over Germany that night, of which total 782 heavy bombers were despatched specifically to destroy Nuremberg. Of these latter, 55 bombers were forced to abort due to a variety of reasons, and of the remainder 636 actually

bombed their objective — or, at least, claimed to have done so in good faith. By early morning the following day, 95 bombers had failed to return, 10 more had reached English shores but crashed and been wrecked, and a further 70 had suffered damage varying in degrees of severity. Of the crews sent to Nuremberg, 745 men had been killed or wounded, 26 others had received injuries, and 159 had been made prisoners of war.

No 5 Group's contribution to this ordeal was an initial total of 202 aircraft despatched, selected from a dozen squadrons. Of these, 10 aborted and 168 claimed to have bombed the target. Next day 21 aircraft had failed to return, and only No 619 Squadron could report no losses in air crew members, despite one Lancaster crashing on return and burning out. It had been a night of triumph for the German defences, in particular the Luftwaffe's night fighter pilots who between them claimed 81 confirmed victories. For the Nachtjäger weather conditions that night were near-perfect, with bright moonlight and little high cloud cover for the bombers. By adding the contemporary ploy of dropping 'fighter flares' above the recognised route of the bomber stream, the German fighter crews virtually operated in conditions of near-daylight visibility in many cases. Moreover, the planned route for the main bomber stream incorporated a long leg which penetrated through a known, well-defended section of Germany for some 260 miles — an open invitation to defending fighter activity.

The full, tragic story of that night is already well documented, and in the context of 5 Group was simply one more 'maximum effort' and in the long 'Battle of Berlin' with higher-than-normal losses and less-than-normal successful results. One crew member who flew to Nuremberg that night exemplifies in many ways the other 5 Group crews who participated, and his particular experience includes events common to many on the raid. D. G. 'Pat' Patfield, a bomb aimer with No 61 Squadron, hailed from Norwich, and was a week away from attaining his majority, his 21st birthday, when his

Left: Flt Sgt D. G. Patfield, No 61
Squadron, 1944.   *D. G. Patfield*

Above: O-Orange of No 61
Squadron.   *D. G. Patfield*

Right: Plt Off Denny Freeman DFC
of No 61 Squadron, 1944.
D. G. Patfield

Far right: Flt Sgt J. Chapman
CGM, No 61 Squadron, 1944.
D. G. Patfield

crew were detailed on the battle order for
Nuremberg:

'Stationed at Coningsby in Lincolnshire, we
were a "green" crew. Seven of us, mostly in
our late 'teens or early twenties. We had
trained together for a number of months previous, with the exception of Tommy, our
navigator, who had crewed up with us only a
week or so before. The experience of being
told "There's a war on tonight and you're on
the list" was therefore received with mixed
feelings, in spite of the fact that during training we'd been anxious to get on with the real
thing.

'The usual business of briefing over, we
were soon clambering aboard QR-Q
"Queenie" out at her dispersal point at the
edge of the airfield, though prior to that we
had all gazed up into the open bomb bay to
have a good look at the bombs hanging there.
We had seen them, or similar ones, before yet
they always fascinated us. In we climbed and
were soon making ourselves as comfortable
as the cramped crew positions would permit.
As we plugged in our intercom we ceased our
somewhat idle chatter — usually about girls
— and got down to the serious job of checking equipment, controls, guns, radio etc, then
waited for the four engines to burst into life.
It wasn't long before we were rumbling
round the perimeter track towards the end of
the runway, accompanied by a queue of other
Lancasters of our squadron which in the
rapidly fading daylight gave the appearance
of large, dark birds of prey. On to the
runway . . . engines revving hard . . . a green
light from the caravan . . . brakes off . . . we
were away.

'Air Ministry Orders had it that "Bomb
Aimers must not sit in the nose of the aircraft
during take-off and landing", or words to
that effect. Anyway, rules are made to be
broken, and having got settled down in the
nose, with maps spread out, parachute
stowed near (*very* near . . .), and the
numerous fairly heavy and bulky brown
covered parcels of Window (anti-radar
metallic foil strips) stacked all around me; it
would have been an effort of a major order to
scramble back through the small opening into
the main cabin, dressed in full flying kit, Mae
West and parachute harness. Within a few
seconds, broken only by the orders of the
pilot and acknowledgments from the flight
engineer, with engines straining to get our
overladen aircraft into the air, the jolting
ceased and, with the engineer's "Undercarriage up", we knew we were really on the

Right: **DV397, QR-W of No 61 Squadron ready to go.
She was lost over Berlin on 24/25 March 1944.** *IWM*

way. With a remark from one crew member, "And to think I had a bloody date in Boston tonight", we settled ourselves to our allotted tasks, en route to Nuremberg. Though we could not know it then, it was to be our last time flying together as a crew.

'Gaining height, we flew off to the rendezvous where we could see the dim shapes of other Lancs turning on to course. Taking up our position, we joined in the gaggle — we didn't fly in formation, indeed it would have been extremely dangerous to have attempted to — and headed for a point on the south-east coast of England on the first leg of the flight plan. Looking down through the perspex blister in the nose, the ground, what could be seen of it, looked strangely peaceful. The main thought in our minds was not whether we would get back all right — you just didn't think of that — but what it would be like at the target, hope we could find it, and then let's get back to that egg, bacon and bed. There wasn't much chatter on the intercom, just the odd remark or two — which usually concentrated on the opposite sex. Every man was intent on his individual tasks, while the two gunners, who always seemed so remote from the rest of the crew, were busy swinging their turrets round, peering into the darkness for anything which shouldn't be there.

'Having put the correct settings on the bombsight computor, I now gazed downwards in the hope of picking up some recognisable landmark which, after checking with a map, could be passed to the navigator as a "pinpoint" to check against his calculated position. Map-reading was the bomb-aimer's primary job, next to actual bombing, and even at night it was surprising how many geographical landmarks could be seen. The hardest part was reading maps as in the nose no lighting was permitted and the only source of light was from a "blacked-out" flashlight with a few tiny pin-pricks to allow a very small percentage of light to pass through. At last the Suffolk coast appeared and on crossing it we really felt we were on our way. Came the usual instruction from the pilot to both gunners, "OK gunners, keep your eyes skinned"!

'Crossing the English coast was always the time for me to prepare the bomb switches for action, and it usually brought a corny remark from someone as I passed my message to the navigator to enter in his log, "All bombs fused and selected"; apparently my Norfolk dialect didn't lend itself kindly to the word "fused" and it sounded like "foozed" — I was therefore usually referred to as a "Swede" or a "Dumpling". After crossing the enemy coast it wasn't long before searchlights were probing the darkness, and then we realised the absence of flak — this we

knew meant one thing — fighters. I immediately started to undo the brown paper parcels of Window and, by means of a small chute in the side of the fuselage, began to throw out the small bundles to disrupt enemy radar defences. It wasn't long before maps, brown paper, string and myself began to get mixed up — the blessed chute wasn't large enough to push the brown paper out as well!

'For the next half-hour or so very little happened, and then came an exchange of machine gun fire over to our port side. It was only a short exchange but suddenly from the same direction we saw a glow in the sky, small at first but soon becoming larger, until we could plainly make out the shape of a Lancaster burning fiercely. It continued flying steadily for a while and then turned and went down in a shallow dive. "Lanc gone down to port!" I yelled to the navigator, whose job it was to log such incidents. It was our first experience of real air combat and with a remark from the pilot, something like "Bugger me! Did you see that? Keep a look-out gunners", I know we all felt that funny feeling in the pit of our stomachs reserved for such occasions. Before long we saw more exchanges of fire. Suddenly the whole sky around us was lit up by what appeared to be huge fireworks — fighter flares. We'd heard all about these during training. They were the things most feared by bomber crews and here they were, hanging in the sky like giant chandeliers of magnesium, being dropped by German aircraft flying above the bomber stream in lanes three or four abreast and stretching out far ahead of us. Other bombers could now be seen clearly on either side and ahead — we felt as naked as the day we were born.

'Very soon combats could be seen taking place all over the sky. Sometimes there followed a ruddy glow lasting only seconds and ending in a terrific explosion. At others, like the first encounter we had seen, the bomber would burn steadily and begin to lose height. These were the lucky ones, or so we thought, as they had time to bale out. In fact we saw two or three parachutes floating down from time to time. "Two going down to port, and one to starboard" I yelled to the navigator. Sometimes, far below — some 20,000 feet in fact — could be seen a large, solitary explosion marking the end of an air-craft, and perhaps its crew, as it hit the ground. Other explosions occurred frequently on the ground, usually a stick of bombs which had been jettisoned from a bomber in distress. Though unavoidable in most cases, these should not have been released until the bomber had turned away from the main stream, because the incendiaries burning on the deck made other bombers stand out clearly to any fighter flying above. The battle raged fiercer, encounters all around us, explosions, fires, and at one time we counted 13 aircraft all going down at the same time. "Gunners, can you see any fighters?" the pilot kept asking; to which the usual reply was "Dozens of the bastards, but none near enough to have a go at". I kept standing up in the front gun turret, just above my head, to man the front guns, But I didn't see anything to have a crack at either.

'Without warning, over the intercom, we heard the gunners firing like mad, and a yell from Bill Smith, the rear gunner, "Look out, skipper" three of "em coming in!" At the same moment there was a terrific explosion and all around things whizzed about. A sickly smell of smoke and cordite, and I was almost thrown on my back as the aircraft tilted at a crazy angle and went into steep dive. My first impressions were of flames around me and my face being very wet and sticky. Blood? — but I felt no pain and seemed to be in one piece. This sticky mess turned out to be hydraulic oil from the gun turret just above my head, as a considerable part of the turret had disappeared and the severed pipes had spewed out their contents over me. We were still diving steeply when the pilot yelled, "I've got her under control but we're in a mess!" The gunners were swearing, and I heard three voices saying rather feebly, "I've been hit" — these were the flight engineer, navigator and wireless operator.

'In the nose I had already pulled aside the rubber cushioning on which I knelt, exposing the emergency hatch in readiness to make a quick exit, but the order didn't come; which was just as well, as I discovered afterwards that the hatch had been chewed up and was wedged fast. Needless to say I'd already hooked on my parachute. "Come up here, Pat" yelled the pilot. I told him I had a bit of a fire amongst the brown paper strewn around me, but fortunately managed to put it out — mainly by sitting on it — then clambered up into the main cabin. Frank Devonshire, the flight engineer, was half-standing, half-kneeling and beating furiously at a glow by his instrument panel; Tommy the navigator, was slumped over the remains of his chart table; while Jimmy Chapman, the wireless operator, was sitting by his set, blood streaming down his face. With some relief I saw that our pilot, Denny Freeman, was apparently unharmed, sitting at his controls, with a shattered windscreen in front of him. "We can still fly", he said, "We've lost a lot of height. I'm turning North, then making for home. Keep a look-out gunners." The engines were still going, though one sounded rough.

'There were no heroic thoughts of pressing on to the target regardless; we didn't know how the fuel tanks had fared, they must be

holed, and many of the fuel gauges on the engineer's panel had been smashed. Besides, we had three wounded on board and the strong instinct of self-preservation ruled. Eventually we got the fires out. These were only in the cabin area and fortunately hadn't got a good hold. "Bomb aimer", we're over Germany so better get rid of the bombs. If we're going down we don't want to take them with us" said the pilot. Clambering back into the nose I pressed the bomb tit — I presumed the skipper had opened the bomb doors! Down they went but as the indicator lamp on the release switches wasn't working, I couldn't tell if they had all gone. Back down the fuselage, still with my parachute on, and I lifted the small inspection covers over the release hooks of each bomb position. One had hung up, the 4,000lb "Cookie". Probing through the small opening with the little length of hooked wire the Air Ministry had kindly supplied for this purpose — known to all as the "Tools, Hooker" — I at last managed to release it.

'The next concern was for the injured. The wireless operator helped me with the navigator. What we took to be a cannon shell had torn a huge hole in his chart table, taking a lot of hand with it. We tied up his arm as best we could and got him to the "rest bed", halfway down the fuselage. We then discovered the escape hatch immediately above the rest bed was missing and an icy blast was coming through, though we didn't give it more thought at the time. Plugging in his oxygen and intercom, I gave him a shot of morphia from the first aid kit, then went back to the flight engineer. The latter was by now about "all in" and sitting on the fuselage floor. His right arm looked a mess and around the elbow his flying suit was badly torn and sticky with blood. My knowledge of first aid being very limited, I was horrified to feel bits of torn flesh and bone and was rather at a loss what to do. Tearing his sleeve open more, I tied a thick bandage near the shoulder as a makeshift tourniquet, gave him a shot of morphia, and tied his arm up in a sling — all this in almost total darkness — then sat him down on the floor behind the pilot. The wireless operator, who had quite a lot of blood on his face, insisted he wasn't badly hurt, but by now he didn't look too good. We decided he had better sit down by his radio and take it easy. This he did but then started fiddling with his set — which bore marks of the engagement — and started getting a radio fix when it was clear to do so, to define our position. From the time of being hit we had forgotten about fighters and in the pandemonium it didn't occur to us that we might be attacked again. It was pure luck that we weren't.

'Being second navigator, among other things, I was then asked by the skipper to see what I could do about navigating us home. The chart table was a shambles, with torn maps, quite a bit of blood about, no protractors or any other navigation instruments to be seen anywhere — this wasn't a bit like the navigation exercises I'd done during training. And the crew was hoping I would get them home! Fortunately, I found the piece of chart showing our last position worked out just prior to our being hit and, knowing we had turned North, and taking roughly the ground speed of the aircraft and approximate time since turning, made a guess at the distance travelled North, then measured this from the scale on the chart with my finger! I was able to put a cross on the chart which looked OK, and judging by eye only, the position of this cross relative to England, and a guess at the drift from the flight plan which I'd also found, enabled me to work out a rough course and pass this to the pilot. Still trying to establish our true position, I was mightily relieved when after a while the wireless operator passed to me a

Below: A clearer view of the havoc created at Mailly Le Camp.

Above: Crew of No 61 Squadron's R5699 on return from Dusseldorf — tired, nerve-strained, but happy to be home again.

Left: Veterans. Lancaster W4236, K-Kitty of A Flight, No 61 Squadron at Syerston on 30 July 1943, displaying a bomb log tally of 72 sorties completed. Its air crew, standing, were (from left): Flt Lt Hewish; Plt Off W. H. Eager; Sgts Stone, Vanner, Petts, Sharrard and Lawrence. With a fresh crew, however, K-Kitty was lost over Mannheim on 9 October 1943.

Below left: A No 57 Squadron crew, on return, check with the maintenance 'Chiefy' before leaving the dispersal for de-briefing.

107

piece of paper with a position written on it. Thank Heaven, he'd got his set to work and obtained an accurate fix. Taking the scrap of paper, I remember having great difficulty in trying to work out which was longitude and which latitude, and trying to plot this fix . . . I didn't succeed . . .

'My next conscious memory was finding myself under the remains of the chart table, and hearing the pilot calling over the R/T, "Mayday! Mayday!" I realised then that we must be over England. I attempted to get up. "Pat's coming round", I heard the wireless operator report as he came to help me up. My head was splitting. "You passed out", said the W/Op, "And you've been out for a long time. You started dancing about soon after I gave you a second fix, then flopped out on the floor. I couldn't see any sign of injury but then saw that your oxygen mask had two fairly big holes in it (shrapnel or bullets, we found out later), so guessed you'd passed out from lack of oxygen, but we daren't come down too low at the time." No wonder it had seemed a short journey home — what a time to sleep! The pilot was still calling "Mayday", then came an answer, "Q-Queenie, searchlights will home you". On my feet now, with nothing worse than a sick headache, I saw from the cabin windows searchlights wavering from the vertical position almost to the ground, like a giant arm beckoning. Following these we saw a cone of three searchlights poised stationary, marking an aerdrome.

'Over the R/T came the controller's voice again, "Q-Queenie, this is Horsham St Faiths. Another plane landing. Do a circuit and land". We almost cried with relief. Again the controller's voice, "Q-Queenie. Runway blocked. Proceed to Foulsham". They gave us a course to fly — Foulsham was only a few minutes' flying time away — and as we seemed to be flying fairly well still, the skipper acknowledged and off we flew. Very shortly we spotted another stationary cone of three searchlights and as we approached we called up Foulsham, who told us it was clear to land. "Undercarriage going down" said the pilot, then "Blast! The indicator isn't working" (This was the green light on his panel when wheels were locked down). The warning horn was sounding, which should have stopped if the wheels were properly locked down. He looked out at the port wheel — that seemed OK — "How about the starboard, Pat?" — this was down but seemed to be flapping about. He swung the aircraft about as much as he dared, hoping to get it to lock, but no joy.

' "Prepare for crash landing. I'm going down." The wireless operator went to the rest bed to hang on to the injured navigator, while I sat down with the engineer with my arm around him to hold him. A sickening lurch as we hit the runway . . . more bumps . . . the skipper was holding the Lanc over on to the port wheel which was apparently locked OK. As we lost flying speed the starboard wing began to drop, then the wing tip dug into the ground, swinging us completely round as we grated to a stop. Our fear now was fire, and getting up we made our way rapidly down the fuselage towards the exit door. The gunners had just opened it when voices were heard shouting, "OK, we'll get you out". Illuminated by headlights from a jeep and an ambulance, we saw some figures climb in to help. Fortunately no fire occurred; poor old Queenie had crumpled quite a bit but, faithful to the end, had not caught fire. Little was said as the injured were taken into the ambulance and off to sick quarters, while the rest of us went by jeep to the briefing room, where a number of officers flocked round us, offering cigarettes and mugs of hot tea with a generous tot of whisky therein. From there, after interrogation, to some Nissen hut and prepared beds.

'Next day we went over to sick quarters to see our injured crew mates but weren't permitted to visit them. The MO (Medical Officer) told us that the wireless operator had quite a lot of small pieces of shrapnel in his back and just under the scalp. The navigator's hand was badly smashed up and (I believe) frost-bitten. I never saw either of them again. The flight engineer's elbow was also badly smashed, and he had quite a number of shrapnel wounds in his side. We then went to have a look at Queenie. There she was, lying out in the middle of the aerodrome, over on to a crumpled wing, her starboard propellers bent back over the engines. We climbed aboard and looked round. What a mess, holes everywhere. How the engines kept going I'll never know. Three German fighters had riddled the old girl, yet she had brought us home. Now she was a write-off. Later that day we were flown back to Coningsby, interrogated, then given a fortnight's leave commencing the next morning.

'Our pilot, Denny Freeman from Gainsborough, was awarded a DFC for bringing the crippled Lanc home safely; while Jimmy Chapman, the wireless operator, was awarded a CGM for getting his set working again, obtaining fixes, plotting them, and helping to navigate after I'd passed out. They were well-deserved awards. Sadly, while flying later with other crews, our two gunners, pilot and wireless opertor were killed. The navigator and flight engineer never flew again. For myself, I completed another 30 operations, though not without incidents, including a collision over Tours on my sixth op on 19 May 1944 . . . but that's another tale.'

Line-Book

'Shooting a line' — boasting of personal qualities or prowess *et al* — was ever a social 'sin' in RAF circles, particularly when it was associated with operations. Though a tiny percentage of line-shooters were, in fact, serious in their remark(s) — and were thus branded for life in their RAF careers, because the 'family grapevine' soon spread their reputation far afield — the vast majority of 'lines' were either entirely unconscious comments, utterly out of true character, or deliberately humorous, if slightly 'edged' with acid intent. Most RAF Messes, especially squadrons, maintained a unit Line Book, in which involuntary 'lines' were faithfully recorded — and necessarily 'witnessed' — for all to read. Such a permanent record of — usually — youthful indiscretions may have caused the odd moment of embarrassment in later years when the original perpetrator returned as a very senior rank and read again his gaffe(s): but the underlying humour and near-gaiety of certain line-books reflected the contemporary light-hearted surface 'balm' in an existence where death and mutilation was ever-near each night on operations. The essence of the very best 'lines' was gross exaggeration — but always spoken with a 'straight' face.

The following 'lines' were recorded in No 9 Squadron's Line-Book during the period 1944-45, though were entirely typical of any squadron throughout the war. If the true humour is not too apparent to the layman, this is because RAF (or any other Service) humour has always been highly esoteric — a traditional mix of bloody-mindedness, fatalism, and accurate observation of RAF life; a 'twisted' humour, in RAF parlance.

28/3/44 Flg Off Mathers:
'You forget, we pilots know *every* job in the aircraft'

28/3/44 Flt Lt Pooley:
(when one of his crew remarked that they should have a photo taken): 'Don't bother, we'll soon get an aiming point'

28/3/44 Flg Off Smith:
'Bombing the Third Reich is my life'

4/4/44 Flt Lt Nancekeville:
'I was in the Unity, Lincoln when you were running around with a white flash in your hat'

5/4/44 Flg Off Smith
(prior to briefing): 'It must be an easy trip tonight, I'm not on the Battle Order'

5/4/44 Flt Lt Brooker:
'I can't remember the day I joined'

9/4/44 Flt Lt Head:
'We've been so busy we haven't had time to get depressed'

9/4/44 Sqn Ldr Keir:
'Breakfast? I never get up late enough for it'

12/3/44 Flt Lt Daniels:
'You Met types can't have a double helping'
Plt Off North:
'Why not? We do double the work'

12/4/44 Plt Off Jeapes:
'My Cookie always puts the marker out. It makes it difficult for the other types'

15/4/44 Flg Off Milward:
'When you've been in the Air Force as long as I have you'll be *entitled* to swear'

16/4/44 Flg Off Smith:
'We bombed the fence round the marshalling yards so that the saboteurs could get in'

18/4/44 Flg Off Manning:
'At Stuttgart I bombed through 7/10ths Lancs'

21/4/44 Plt Off Stafford:
'I don't use *George* because when I get my hands and feet settled on the controls it's just like *George*'

24/4/44 Flg Off Prior:
'There's nobody here I can talk to — they're all sprogs'

24/4/44 Flg Off Mitchell:
'We don't like bombing too high in case we hit a Halifax'

28/4/44 Flg Off Manning:
'No Battle Order is complete without my name on it'

28/4/44 Plt Off Lasham:
'We can't carry too many bombs in S-S-hambles, or we should hit all the Lancs underneath'

28/4/44 Plt Off Lasham:
'We only use four motors to get airborne — we cut the outers after take-off'

30/4/44 Flg Off Mitchell
(Nobby Clarke's Nav after a 95° error): 'When we are detailed to aim at a boiler house, we pick out the safety valves'

10/5/44 Plt Off Craig:
'I don't do any corrections. I just get the red spot fire lined up on the run and the bomb aimer has nothing to do'

10/5/44 Flt Lt Mathers:
'I was being so careful that I re-trimmed the aircraft after each bomb'

4/5/44 Flg Off Gross:
'We were so low at times that we couldn't see over the top of the waves'

14/3/44 Sect Off Kipps, WAAF
(discussing pay) remarked that a Pilot Officer was paid higher than a Section Officer whereupon Plt Off Sartori replied, 'Well, I earn it'

2/6/44 Flg Off Lewis:
'When I first started ops we had to blow our whistles to get a QDM'

8/8/44 Flg Off Lewis
(after last trip of second tour): 'I work so hard that today I was finding winds over England on the way home — it's a habit'

15/8/44 Wg Cdr Bazin
(after his bombing at Brest on 13 August): 'Group tell me that I can take the rest of the squadron tomorrow, just as support'

21/8/44 Sqn Ldr Keir
(after last trip of second tour): 'Oh yes. I've seen the time when the vis was so bad that after a pilot landed he had to get QDMs to the Watch Office'

26/3/45 Flt Lt Jones:
'Flak? You see my hat — faded from the bloody searchlights in the Ruhr'

Other 'lines' — selected from various squadrons' line-books, at varying periods of the war — include the following gems:

'Oh, I just tell my bomb-aimer to bomb through a hole in the flak'

'The flak was so bloody thick, I daren't put my hand out of the window'

'It's all right for navigators in Mossies: we fly so low we can always get out and ask the way'

'My skipper's so fussy about accuracy he does a run-in for *every* bomb'

'Not Essen again. I'm sick of that place' (after speaker had completed just one op)

'I've flown Q-Queenie to the Ruhr so often, she knows her own way home now'

'When I first joined Pontius was still at OTU'

'My gunners are so good I don't know what a corkscrew is'

'That Jerry fighter was so bloody close I could read *his* instruments'

'My aiming is so accurate the briefing zobbitt has to tell me which number in the street to hit'

'We've been to Berlin so often my nav doesn't bother with a map'

'When the second engine packed up I thought of getting out and walking home on the flak'

'I've had so many ops-eggs, I go to sleep with my head under my arm'

'It comes to something when the Master of Ceremonies corrects *my* bombing'

'Aiming Point photos? Are there any other sort?'

'We came home so low my nav was reading road-signs'

'When I first joined the Command we all knew each other'

'Born leaders? No, there aren't many of us'

Far right, top: **With Cpl V. Carter WAAF listening-out at the Patrol Handling Board, the Waddington Station commander, Grp Capt Bonham-Carter (nearest) and others anxiously wait for the return of Lancaster R5868, PO-S, of No 467 Squadron RAAF from Bourg-Leopold, ostensibly the veteran bomber's 100th sortie of the war, on 12 May 1944.** *Central Press*

Far right, bottom: **By July 1943 more than 7,000 WAAF airwomen were employed in operations rooms, as watchkeepers etc, but less than 200 WAAF officers were employed on Intelligence duties in all capacities. Using WAAF officers to interrogate returning aircrews was, at first, considered 'inadvisable psychologically' by higher authorities; but by 1944 they were familiar figures at de-briefings. Typical scene is this crew at Swinderby on 23 November 1943 on return from Berlin.** *IWM*

Right: **A wartime Chris Wren cartoon which hardly needs comment ...**

." —approaching the target, showers of—er—stuff came up—we jinked like—er—anything, which completely— er—er—messed up our bombing run—we turned and dropped the whole bl—inking load through a hole in the flak ! "

Above: Back from Stuttgart, the crew of B-Bertie is 'de-briefed' by an ex-London dancing teacher WAAF officer.

Right: No 630 Squadron crew of ME739, D-Dog happy to be back at East Kirkby after bombing some French rail yards on 18 April 1944. *IWM*

Far right, top: LL744, VN-B of No 50 Squadron, January 1944, usually piloted by Flt Lt Mike Beetham (now Chief of the Air Staff). *L. Bartlett*

Far right, bottom: Flt Lt M. Beetham DFC (centre, standing) and his No 50 Squadron crew.
Courtesy OC No 50 Squadron RAF

Left: Back from the long haul to Milan, a gaggle of No 50 Squadron crews pose for the Press, 1943.

Below left: An off-duty moment at Swinderby, 1942. Standing: Flt Lt Martin Smith; Hugh Everitt DSO, DFC; Jack Leggo; Eve Vanderbilt and her mother; Fay Gillam (WAAF officer). Nearest camera Bob Hay, Resplendent in borrowed 'Groupie's' hat, puts the finger on Micky Martin.
Courtesy OC No 50 Squadron RAF

Right: Three No 50 Squadron members — Sgt A. Penfold, Plt Off H. Gilleland and R. C. 'Bob' Hay — studying a Swinderby signpost. All three were to die within the year.
Courtesy OC No 50 Squadron RAF

Below: No 50 Squadron ground crews in front of Lancaster ME596, VN-H, at Skellingthorpe. Later 'H' of No 61 Squadron, this Lanc was lost over Russelsheim on 12/13 August 1944.

Right: Flt Lt Jim Cowan DFC of No 9 Squadron, Waddington, circa December 1942, with a 15-ops bomb log, including seven to Italian targets as denoted by ice-cream cones. *L. Brown*

Below: No 9 Squadron's Battle Honours board. The motto — 'There's always bloody something' — was derived from the favourite remark of a famous ex-Flight commander, Grp Capt P. C. Pickard DSO, DFC who gained legendary fame in the Amiens Gaol raid of 1944.

Pride~
in Paint

Above: **An appropriate 'Indian and tomahawks' ops log for Sqn Ldr W. J. Burnett's Hampden of No 408 Squadron RCAF at Syerston on 30 September 1941.** *Public Archives of Canada*

Right: Sri Gajah — Jill; the insigne of Flt Lt R. A. Fletcher DFC, DFM's Lancaster with No 97 Squadron. *IWM*

Below: No 9 Squadron's famous W4964, WS-J, *Johnny Walker* which eventually completed 106 ops; seen here with Flt Lt Doug Melrose (far left) and his crew, September/October 1944.

Below right: ED611, *Uncle Joe*, of No 463 Squadron RAAF which totted up a total of at least 115 operational sorties by the end of the war — 43 of these with No 44 Squadron initially. *L. Cottroll*

Bottom left: ME701, JO-F, *Whoa Bessie* of No 463 Squadron RAAF, pictured at Waddington on 1 March 1944. *RAAF*

Right: LL636, a Lanc BII of No 408 Squadron RCAF in June 1944. Airmen are from top: left — LAC Harry Truax, LAC Harvey Arnold and Sgt Jeff Godfrey. Right — LAC Bob Ferry (in cockpit), LAC Keith Cinnamon, Sgt Sam McCracken and LAC Gordon Palin. The use of the official squadron badge as decoration was rare.
Public Archives of Canada

Below: LL725, *Z-Zombie* of No 408 Squadron RCAF at Linton-on-Ouse on 24 April 1944. Her usual skipper was Flg Off E. M. C. Franklin.
Public Archives of Canada

Above: A few of the A&E ground crews of No 619 Squadron at Strubby, 1944 with Lanc 'N', *The Weasel*, displaying a log of 66 ops. *F. Slater*

Above right: *Naughty Nan* of No 9 Squadron at Bardney, 1944, with Jock Keir and his crew after completing the last sortie of their tour. From left: Bob Gross; Shepherd; Jock Keir; Arthur Dearden; 'Griff'.

Right: Armourer takes a rest on the SBC load of incendiaries while refuelling is completed.

Below right: LL844, JO-R of No 463 Squadron RAAF. *P. H. T. Green*

121

Right: Ton-up. The veteran ED588, VN-G which ultimately flew 126 sorties, 118 of these with No 50 Squadron. It was then lost on 29/30 August 1944.
Courtesy OC No 50 Squadron RAF

Below: Barbara Mary — a No 9 Squadron Lancaster flown by Flt Lt Jim Cowan DFC from Waddington in late 1942. The name-plate was a carry-over of the names applied to his former No 9 Squadron Wellington.
L. Brown

Bottom: LL842, VN-F, of No 50 Squadron commemorates the well-known wartime striptease artiste Phyllis Dixey.
D. Richardson DFC

Left: ED860, N-Nan of No 61 Squadron completes her 100th sortie — flown on 30 June 1944. *IWM*

Below: Another No 50 Squadron Lanc, at Skellingthorpe, 'belonging' to Len Durham's crew. *J. P. Flynn*

Above: Four delightful decorations applied to various Lancasters of No 9 Squadron.

Right: D-Dumbo of No 619 Squadron on the A Flight dispersal at Strubby, winter 1944–45. *F. Slater*

124

Left: A kneeling nude, with bomb, was the insigne initially applied to Lanc B1, R5868, PO-S, on its first arrival on No 467 Squadron RAAF. The initial operations were then flown by this crew Standing — W. Booth (nav), Steve Bethell (MU/AG), Ken Worden (rear AG) and A. Martin (flt/eng). Kneeling: W. Griffin (B/A), N. McClelland (captain), and S. Bray (W/Op).
D. Miller

Below: Beers and cheers. Air and ground crews of No 467 Squadron RAAF at Waddington on 12 May 1944, saluting the 100th completed ops sorties of Lancaster R5868, *S-Sugar* the previous night. On the 'platform of honour' are Flg Off T. N. Scholefield and his crew who flew the trip. *RAAF*

Sink the Tirpitz

On 5 November 1937 the leader of the German nation, Hitler, assembled his Service chiefs at the Berlin Chancellery, in secret, for a dissertation on his personal political objectives for the Third Reich. Naming England as the 'hateful enemy', Hitler made it crystal clear to his audience that his eventual intention was war, and that his fighting services were to commence preparations accordingly. In particular he ordered the *Kriegsmarine* (Navy) to provide him with a Fleet capable of challenging the British Royal Navy, with the result that the 'Z-Plan Fleet' programme of naval construction was underway in the following year. In December 1938 the first of the Z-Plan 'super' ships was launched — the aircraft carrier *Graf Zeppelin* — to be followed in early 1939 by two super-battleships, the *Tirpitz* and the *Bismarck*. This pair of sister ships were the largest, fastest battleships ever built to date; huge, elegant vessels packed with massive armament and radar facilities. Each was of 42,000 tons — the *Tirpitz* having a tonnage

of 52,600 when fully laden and thus heavier than its stable-mate — and could steam at 31 knots. Each carried a crew of 2,400 officers and ratings, and mounted eight 15-inch guns in a quartet of twin turrets, while *Tirpitz* (unlike the *Bismarck*) also had torpedo tubes mounted amidships. Each ship was unquestionably a triumph of naval engineering, and — significantly — each could outpace any ship in the contemporary Royal Navy.

With the outbreak of war in September 1939 Hitler effectively nullified the Z-Plan programme. His Kriegsmarine was far from equipped to the intended strength for an international war — the plan could not have been fully implemented for at least six more years — and found itself committed to hostilities with, in the main, a fleet existing only on paper. Both the *Bismarck* and the *Tirpitz* had yet to complete necessary exhaustive trials before being considered operationally ready; while the British navy outnumbered the existing German Fleet by a

Below: A 12,000lb MC 'Tallboy' aboard its Type H trolley at Bardney bomb dump on 9 September 1944. With its No 78 Tail Unit fitted (as here) the overall length was 21ft, with a maximum bomb body diameter of 3ft 2in. Actual explosive filling was approx 5,200lb of Torpex D1 — a Charge/Weight Ratio (CWR) of 44%. Fused at the tail end only, the 'Tallboy' used either three No 58 pistols or three No 47 long-delay pistols; the latter offering either half an hour or an hour's delay in actual detonation of the explosive filling.

Above: Winching up. The Type H Trolley was provided with four 6,000lb bomb winches integrally, mounted on a modified Type E Trolley with reinforced steel superstructure.

Left: Ready to go. Hoisted and secured.

Above: Lancaster B1 (Special) of No 617 Squadron, loaded with a 22,000lb 'Grand Slam' bomb revs hard prior to take-off. The 'Grand Slam' was (basically) a scaled-up 'Tallboy'; being 4.5ft longer and eight inches fatter in body diameter. The main explosive filling comprised 9,135lb of Torpex D1 — a CWR of approx 42%. *IWM*

factor of approximately eight-to-one. Grossadmiral Erich Raeder, as head of the Kriegsmarine then, was faced with an uphill task. Expected to produce resounding naval victories by Hitler — who had little interest or knowledge in naval affairs — yet without the necessary strength, equipment or sheer numbers in vessels with which to achieve superiority. Hoarding his precious 'super-ships', like a gambler down to his last handful of blue chips, Raeder finally permitted the *Bismarck* to sail into the open Atlantic on 18 May 1941, in company with the *Prinz Eugen* and attendant escort vessels, for Operation 'Rheinübung' ('Rhine Exercise') a foray against Allied shipping. Clashing with HMS *Hood* and the *Prince of Wales* six days later, the *Bismarck's* guns sank the *Hood* and damaged the *Prince of Wales*, but met its own death shortly before noon on 27 May. The *Tirpitz*, prevented from being included in 'Rheinübung' because her official trials had yet to be completed, was eventually sent to a berth in Norwegian waters in January 1942, at Foettenfjord, nr Trondheim. Here, safely berthed only 40 miles from the open sea, the battleship was poised on the perimeter of the vast Atlantic battlefield; a grey menace over-shadowing all Allied naval movements. Recognising the threat, Winston Churchill wrote to the Admiralty, 'The destruction or even crippling of this ship is the greatest event at sea at the present time. No other target is comparable to it. I regard the matter as of the highest urgency and importance.'

From the date of the *Tirpitz's* arrival in Norway the ship became the objective of a continuing series of attacks by sea and air, including 15 separate attacks by aircraft from the Fleet Air Arm and Bomber Command, during the following two and a half years. In addition were several attempts by specialised craft from the Royal Navy, employing midget submarines and X-craft. All of these attacks caused damage in varying degrees of severity, but none actually sank the *Tirpitz*, which remained a threatening presence, ever ready to pounce on Allied convoys. The simple fact that the battleship was, to all intents, avail-able for sea operations forced the Admiralty to maintain a watch-and-ward force of ships on the spot; ships which could better have been employed in other theatres of war. Dis-cussions by the Allied Joint Planning Staff in the early summer of 1944 reached the con-clusion that the only feasible weapons which could pierce the *Tirpitz's* armoured plating were the giant 12,000lb 'Tallboy' bombs and, possibly, the 4/500lb 'Johnny Walker' mines — the latter for under-keel explosions. By August 1944 the German raider was berthed in Alten Fjord — just beyond the range of any Lancaster loaded with a 'Tallboy' based in Britain. Accordingly, a request was sent to Moscow for suitable airfields and facilities for Lancasters in order that a form of 'shuttle service' could be employed; permitting the bombers to land in Russia after bombing, refuel, then fly back to Britain. The site eventually selected was a grass field at Yagodnik, on an island in the River Dvina, some 20 miles south of Archangel.

On 7 September the Air Staff issued Operation 'Paravane' — the plan to sink the *Tirpitz* by a force of Lancasters, using both 'Tallboys' and 'Johnny Walkers'. Com-manded overall by Grp Capt C. C. McMullen, the force comprised a total of 38

Above: Bomb gone. A 'Grand Slam' on the point of release from Lanc YZ-C of No 617 Squadron during an attack on the Arnsberg Bridge on 19 March 1945. To accommodate this huge explosive store, lightening the normal Lancaster airframe included deletion of the mid-upper and nose gun turrets; the locations of which were then somewhat crudely faired over (as can be seen here). *IWM*

Centre left: Going down. The tail unit incorporated four stub aerofoils, each set at five degrees angle to the bomb centre-line, to provide necessary spin to the bomb in flight and thus increasing the trajectory accuracy. This particular 'Tallboy' was being dropped on 19 June 1944. *IWM*

Bottom left: Lancaster YZ-B of No 617 Squadron over the Arbergen Bridge on 21 March 1945. *IWM*

129

Lancasters drawn almost equally from No 617 Squadron at Woodhall Spa and No 9 Squadron at nearby Bardney, plus two Liberators from No 151 Squadron to convey ground crews and gear to Yagodnik, a PRU Mosquito, and a No 463 Squadron Lancaster, LM587, to film the action. All crews were briefed on 8 September by 5 Group's AOC, Ralph Cochrane, and on 11 September all 42 aircraft left Bardney to fly to Lossiemouth, Scotland. After refuelling here, the force set out for a non-stop flight to Russia, though one Lancaster was forced to return early, having jettisoned its 'Tallboy' due to faulty anchorage of the bomb. Over Russian soil the force ran into thick cloud which, combined with inadequate maps and faulty signals identification of the Yagodnik beacon, led to several Lancasters going astray. Only 24 Lancasters actually landed at Yagodnik — the remaining aircraft were scattered around the Russian countryside, including two from No 617 Squadron (EE131

and ME559) which had force-landed in marshes and, along with four other Lancs from No 9 Squadron which had met similar fates, were eventually abandoned in situ. Others had suffered minor damage, including NE920 which had strayed over Finland and been hit by flak, but the ground crews immediately set to work to prepare all available aircraft for the attack, working non-stop for the next 48 hours in primitive conditions and lacking adequate maintenance facilities on the 'airfield'.

On the morning of 15 September the attack commenced. The first Lancaster became airborne at 0630hrs and within 23 minutes a further 27 Lancasters had left the Yagodnik field. Six aircraft were loaded with 'Johnny Walker' mines, but the rest carried a 'Tallboy' each, with the exception of the film Lanc. The No 9 Squadron element — 10 crews — were led by the squadron commander Wg Cdr J. M. Bazin DFC, while No 617's crews were led by Wg Cdr J. B.

Below: **The first operational use of Barnes Wallis's 12,000lb 'Tallboys' was on the night of 8/9 June 1944, 48 hours after D-Day, when a total of 19 bombs were dropped by No 617 Squadron Lancasters on the Saumur tunnel to block the reinforcement German tanks due to move to the Allied beachheads in Normandy. The target was accurately marked by Leonard Cheshire, then utterly destroyed by the Lancaster force, which included one flown by Bill Reid VC.**

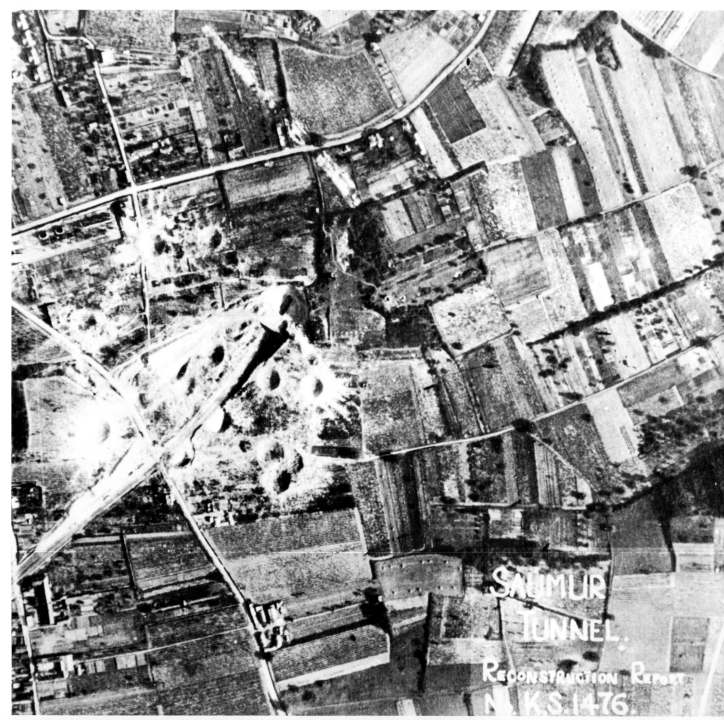

SAUMUR
TUNNEL.
RECONSTRUCTION REPORT
NKS 1476

'Willie' Tait DSO, DFC, in Lancaster EE146. The flight plan called for an attack from south of the *Tirpitz* — in the hope of an element of surprise — and the 'Tallboy' aircraft were to bomb in four waves of five aircraft in line-abreast formation, with only a few hundred yards between each wave. The 'Johnny Walker' force were to bomb at a lower altitude, crossing the target from south-east to north-west. Weather over the target approach area was found to be almost ideal, with only a little low stratus cloud, and the defensive smoke screen only commenced six or seven minutes before Tait made the initial attack. As the tip of the *Tirpitz's* foremast came into Tait's bomb aimer's sight, Tait let go the giant 'Tallboy'; to be followed within seconds by the rest of the Lancaster formations' bombs in steady succession. Smoke had by then obscured the target outline, but the bomb aimers succeeded in plastering the immediate target area. In all 17 'Tallboys' were released, plus the follow-up 'Johnny Walker' mines, but no crew member could be certain of a hit or even a near-miss due to the smoke 'umbrella' over the battleship and its moorings. There was no fighter opposition, but flak damaged two Lancasters and both aircraft managed to return safely to Yagodnik. The only loss was a No 617 aircraft, PB416, skippered by Flg Off F. Levy which (presumably) crashed among the Norwegian mountains. Four Lancs failed to release their 'Tallboys', and one of these, captained by Flg Off M. Scott of No 9 Squadron, made four runs attempting to let go his bomb without success — only to have it fall off of its own accord just before he reached Jagodnik.

While most of the Lancasters returned to England on the following day, the PR Mosquito spent five more days trying to obtain photographic evidence of the attack results, and finally returned on 20 September with

131

film showing that, although not sunk, the battleship had been damaged. What the photographs failed to reveal, however, was the true extent of that damage. Tait's 'Tallboy' had hit the *Tirpitz's* bows, passed through the ship's side, and exploded beneath the keel. The resulting hole in the foc'sle — some 30ft deep by 50ft long — let in 1,000 tons of water. Two following bombs had registered near-misses, wrecking the armoured deck, putting the main engines out of action, and destroying most fire-control instrumentation. The mighty *Tirpitz* was crippled for the rest of its life. Hasty and temporary repairs were effected to its bows and on 15 October, on Admiral Dönitz's order, the ship steamed 200 miles southwards at a crawling seven knots, and eventually berthed in shallow waters in the lee of Haaköy Island, three miles from Tromsö on the following day. Her intended purpose now was solely as a defensive floating gun battery against any possible invasion of Norway by the Allies — still one of Hitler's chief fears despite the invasion of France months earlier. By moving the ship that far south Donitz had, unwittingly, sealed its fate, because Tromsö could be reached by suitably modified Lancasters from UK bases.

Strictly speaking, there was no further purpose in attacking the *Tirpitz*. In its crippled state it was no longer a threat to any form of Allied activity, and might well have been left to rust in peace. Allied intelligence already knew that the ship had moved south, and were also well aware that a force of Luftwaffe fighters had been moved in to the nearby airfield at Bardufoss. Nevertheless, the long-held obsession with the *Tirpitz's* potential led the Admiralty to assume that the ship's move to Tromsö was merely a stopping-stage of a move to German dockyards where it might be fully repaired and made ready again for sea-going action. The decision was taken to lay on a repetition of the September sortie, using the same two squadrons, Nos 617 and 9, with 'Tallboys'; only this time they would fly from Lossiemouth direct to the target, bomb and

return to Scotland. Eighteen Lancasters each from both units were flown to Lossiemouth, all mid-upper gun turrets and armour plating removed, and extra fuel tanks were installed. All Merlin engines were changed to be replaced by Merlin 24 powerplants to give the best possible take-off 'urge' with over-load. By 28 October all aircraft were ready for the raid — again to be led by Tait and Bazin — and early next morning all 36, plus a photographic-film Lanc, took off in blinding rain at approximately 0300hrs, with a six hours' leg to the target. On arrival the crews found the ship covered by low cloud and had to bomb 'blind', dropping a total of 32 'Tallboys'. No fighters came up to meet them, but flak was heavier than on the previous occasion, and one Lancaster — the same NF920 which had suffered hits in the first raid — was hit over the target and subsequently force-landed in neutral Sweden.

On return to Lossiemouth the crews made no claims for any direct hits, yet unbeknown to them one near-miss had distorted the ship's port propeller shaft and rudder, resulting in extensive flooding along the port side aft — the ship could no longer steam under its own power. Both squadrons returned to their normal base airfields but their aircraft remained modified, awaiting the next opportunity to finally sink the *Tirpitz*. On 10 November the order was issued to return to Lossiemouth, and by noon the next day the force had begun refuelling and arming. In the early hours of 12 November, a total of 39 Lancasters revved up engines for take-off, and at 0300hrs the first bomber got airborne. Only 31 others followed, seven of No 9 Squadron's aircraft failing to get away due to frost and icing problems. Leaving the UK via a flashing red beacon on North Unst, the tip of Shetland, the Lancasters flew individual courses towards Norway, led yet again by 'Willie' Tait, in EE146, 'D', with Sqn Ldr A. G. Williams leading the No 9 Squadron element. The flight plan was for all aircraft to rendezvous over a distinctly-shaped lake some 100 miles from Tromsö, form up there, and proceed to the target. By dawn the

YOU BUILT THE MACHINES THEY SANK THE TIRPITZ.

TIRPITZ—THE LAST PHASE

TELEGRAM RECEIVED FROM M.A.P. LONDON. 9.00 A.M. 15th. NOVEMBER, 1944.

FOLLOWING MESSAGE TO YOUR WORKS FROM WING COMMANDER J.B. TAIT, D.S.O.,

D.S.C., WHO LED THE ATTACK ON THE TIRPITZ.

"THE SINKING OF THE TIRPITZ LAST SUNDAY IS AN ACHIEVEMENT OF WHICH YOU

WHO BUILT THE LANCASTERS HAVE EVERY RIGHT TO FEEL PROUD. AN AIRCRAFT WHICH

CAN CARRY 12,000LB BOMBS TO THE ARCTIC CIRCLE, A MUCH LONGER FLIGHT THAN

TO BERLIN, AND STAND UP TO ALL THE GUNS OF A BATTLESHIP, IS A TRIUMPH OF

BRITISH DESIGN AND WORKMANSHIP."

YOUR LANCASTERS P.D. 368 AND D.V. 391 TOOK PART.

—'We knew Tirpitz was done'

Britain, Canada and Australia

HERE are five of the six R.A.F. officers who came to London yesterday to tell the detailed story of the sinking of the Tirpitz.

In the picture above are Squadron-Leader A. G. Williams, of Cirencester, second-in-command, aged 31, Flying-Officer Dennis Nolan, bomb-aimer, and Flight-Lieutenant Eric Giersch, 30, rear-gunner in the film-taking plane.

Nolan, of Forest Hill, London, is pictured again, on the right.

To the left of this caption you see Flying-Officer Walter A. Daniel, D.F.C. aged 24, of Maryleboe, and on the extreme left, Flight-Lieutenant B. A. Buckham, aged 28, of Australia, whose Lancaster filmed the attack. He estimated there were four direct hits on the Tirpitz. "I thought she was never going to sink," he said.

Lancasters were over Norway, and as one pilot described the scene, 'It was the most beautiful morning, with mountains and snow and frozen lakes as far as you could see.' The early morning weather conditions were perfect with clear, cloudless skies and no winds, while visibility stretched miles ahead — ideal conditions for a precision raid. Tait reached the rendezvous lake, circuited once, then led the force towards Tromsö.

At 20 miles range the *Tirpitz* could be seen — unprotected by hills, naked in open water. At 15 miles the first opposition came up as the ship's main armament commenced firing at the oncoming formation of black bombers, but no aircraft wavered. Though still out of range, two flakships nearby, the *Nymph* and the *Thetis*, added their guns to the furious barrage from *Tirpitz* — and still the bombers bore in. At 0940hrs the first 'Tallboys' were seen to leave their aircraft, spinning down, and straddling the ship's anchorage. In all 28 bombs were dropped, and one of the first — thought to be the 'Tallboy' released from Terry Playford's No 617 Squadron Lanc — hit the ship's B Turret; while a second hit amidships on the aircraft catapult along the port side. Two others landed in the water close to the port side and tore a gaping hole in the ship's side, flooding the innards with thousands of tons of water. Within seconds the huge battleship was listing nearly 20 degrees to port, and in less than four minutes was listing by nearly 40 degrees. At 0950, or thereabouts, listing to a crazy angle of some 70 degrees, the C Turret erupted in flame as ammunition stocks detonated and ignited. Two minutes later the vessel was completely on its side in the water.

The whole attack lasted just three minutes. As the last Lancaster droned into the distance, the *Tirpitz* finally capsized, turning completely over in the shallow water, and trapping nearly 1,000 men inside her ruptured hull. Subsequent rescue operations managed to retrieve 87 men from inside the hull, while some 600 others of the ship's crew were rescued from the surrounding waters. Fatal casualties totalled some 900 sailors killed, drowned or stifled to death. The sole 'casualty' to the bombers was one Lancaster, LM448, which force-landed in Sweden, one of No 9 Squadron's aircraft on its 24th operational sortie. Confirmation of the ship's destruction was radioed to England by a Norwegian underground worker that same night; while a PR Mosquito brought back photographic evidence the next day. The ship's epitaph was contained in a German signal sent: 'From Naval Communications Officer Tromsö to Naval Group North, Flag Officer, Norway. *Tirpitz* blown up and capsized 0946/12/44.'

133

Marker Mossies

Below: **Mosquito DZ484, AZ-G of No 627 Squadron with its crew Wg Cdr J. R. 'Benny' Goodman DFC (right) and his navigator, Flg Off A. J. L. 'Bill' Hickox.** *Grp Capt J. R. Goodman DFC, AFC*

On the night of 25/26 June 1942, a total of 1,006 bombers were despatched to attack the Focke-Wulf factories at Bremen — the third and ultimate '1,000-bomber' raid laid on by 'Butch' Harris in his successful ploy to retain Bomber Command as a separate entity to pursue a future strategic offensive against Germany. Of that main force 15 were Avro Manchesters, one of which (L7289 of No 50 Squadron) failed to return. It was the swan song of the ill-starred Manchester, and although each unit temporarily retained three or four examples for crew training and conversion to the bigger, better Lancaster, none saw further operational use. From July 1942, therefore, 5 Group became an all-Lancaster group in terms of heavy bomber equipment. Some two years later, however, 5 Group acquired a handful of Mosquito bombers to act as a 'private' marking force for their main bomber forces; a form of low-level marking technique pioneered within the Group by Leonard Cheshire with No 617 Squadron. The latter unit remained a 'special' Lancaster squadron in the main, but retained a few Mosquitos for the low marking role; and the only 5 Group squadron to be fully Mosquito-equipped was No 627. One of its earliest members was J. R. 'Benny' Goodman (now, Group Captain, DFC, AFC, RAF Retd), whose experiences in the Mossie-marker role reflect those of the other 627 and 617 Mosquito crews:

'No 627 Squadron was formed on 24 November 1943 by the simple expedient of posting C Flight of No 139 Squadron from Wyton to Oakington that day and giving them a new squadron numberplate. Whenever a new squadron was formed in Bomber Command it was a standing requirement that the new unit should be on the Battle Order as quickly as possible, and thus No 627 was briefed for operations that same night. Four crews stood by but in the event only one took off, DZ615 (a Mk IV), piloted by myself with Flg Off A. J. L. "Bill" Hickox as navigator. The target was Berlin and the sortie proved to be uneventful. Only when we returned to base did we learn that DZ615 had been the only Bomber Command aircraft out that night. [These two officers were to become No 627 Squadron's first DFC awards, in April 1944 . . . Author].

'During the winter of 1943-44 "Bill" and I took part in many sorties with No 627 Squadron as part of the Light Night Striking Force (LNSF) belonging to 8 (PFF) Group. However, the role of the squadron was changed in the spring of 1944 as a result of events which were taking place in 5 Group, which occupied the chain of airfields in Lincolnshire. All squadrons tried to attack targets accurately and some were better at this than others. 5 Group achieved striking results in precision attacks, of which the most memorable was the Dams raid in early 1943, carried out by No 617 Squadron. When Wg Cdr Leonard Cheshire took command of No 617 Squadron he brought precision bombing to a new high level of achievement by destroying small but important targets such as factories, finding and marking them at night in Lancasters. He soon realised that the marking problem would be eased if a more manoeuvrable aircraft were used, and permission was obtained to "borrow" two Mosquitos from 8 Group and to attempt marking with them. It was found that great accuracy could be achieved if the Mosquito dived on the target from about 2,000ft at about 30 degrees, and the pilot dropped the marker while the aircraft was pointing at the target ie no bomb sight was employed. This proved to be a turning point, or a major jump, in the technique of marking targets, and it must not be forgotten that the "architect" was Leonard Cheshire.

'The AOC of 5 Group, AVM Cochrane, was quick to appreciate that if one Mosquito could mark a target for a squadron, then a squadron of these aircraft should be able to mark targets for his whole Group. After negotiations at high level it was decided that No 627 Squadron should be moved from Oakington to Woodhall Spa where No 617 was located. The squadron deployed to Woodhall on 13 April 1944 and was officially "detached" from 8 Group, as were Nos 83 and 97 Lancaster squadrons which were to become the flare-dropping force whose job would be to identify and illuminate targets by H2S radar and to lay a carpet of flares, under which the Mosquitos would seek and mark the targets visually. Both Nos 83 and 97 Squadrons deployed from their 8 Group bases to Coningsby, next door to Woodhall Spa.

'After No 627 had landed at Woodhall each crew was welcomed personally by the AOC. We knew then that we were in for something unusual — and probably bloody dangerous! The next thing that happened was a briefing at Coningsby, at which the method of marking targets at low level was explained. We then returned to Woodhall and for ten days practised dive-bombing at the Wainfleet range in the Wash. It was not long before we discovered, as Cheshire had said, that the Mosquito was "just the job" for this technique and we all achieved very good results — often popping the practice bombs right alongside the target. Our "freshman" trip took place on 20 April, when we flew to La Chappelle railway yards, with No 617 leading the way and showing us how the job was done. We then went to Brunswick, Munich (the trip that put the seal of approval on Leonard Cheshire's VC), and on 26 April to

Schweinfurt (on which I flew DZ615 again). Munich was very lively and, relatively, a very long trip — over five hours — while Schweinfurt was not one of the better trips; we had one hell of a job to find the place owing to the murk. For these trips No 617 led the way and we acted as "backers up", concentrating our markers on top of those dropped by the experts. I should, however, explain a function performed by the Flare Force on behalf of the Mosquito markers. The point is that the Mosquitos had only Gee as a navigational aid, and this was jammed by the Germans as soon as Bomber Command took off. The result was that Mosquito navigators could use Gee only as far as the Dutch coast or a short distance into France. We would therefore navigate by dead reckoning (DR) to a point about 10 miles short of the target, where the Flare Force Lancasters would lay a couple of yellow target indicators (TIs). We would fly to these indicators and set course from them to the target; a system which worked very well. However, by the beginning of May we were ready to mark targets for 5 Group, leaving No 617 to carry out its "special" tasks as laid down by higher authority.

'Our first "solo" took place on 1 May 1944, with four Mosquitos of No 627 and the Lancaster Flare Force visiting the Usine Lictard Works at Tours. This was during the time when the Americans were doing high-level "precision" daylight bombing in their B-17 and B-24 aircraft, using the Norden bombsight. Their contention was that they could drop a pickle into a barrel from 30,000 feet with this bombsight, and they called it "pickle-barrel bombing". Well, the Usine Lictard Works had been attacked in this way several days before we went there, and it was evident from the photos taken afterwards that the "pickles" had jumped out of the "barrel" — the works were virtually intact, but there were many holes in the surrounding fields.

'All that day we studied maps and photographs of the area around Tours in which the works lay. Thus, when the flares ignited above the target, we were quickly there searching for the target itself. The technique required that the first marker pilot to find the target was to call "Tally-Ho" on his VHF radio, and the other marker aircraft would then move a short distance away in order to give him elbow-room. On this occasion I was the one to see the target first and I called, "Pen-nib 37, Tally-Ho", easing around the factory and into a position from which I could carry out a shallow dive on to the centre of the target. It worked like a charm, and within a few seconds red spot fires had been dropped on the glass roof of the machine shop. Unfortunately, however, the

Above: **Low-level marking. Incendiary marker dropped by Leonard Cheshire's Lancaster of No 617 Squadron from 200ft bursting over the Gnome-Rhone factory at Limoges on 8/9 February 1944. The dark blob at top centre is the Lanc's tail-wheel.**
Courtesy OC No 617 Squadron RAF

markers disappeared *inside* the shop and could only be seen from directly above. This was an important lesson for us all, namely that the object of our efforts was not to drop our marker bombs *on* the target, but near it in a position where the red blob could be clearly seen by the main force trundling behind. On this occasion Marker Leader flew over the top and directed another Mosquito to drop his markers in the yard alongside the machine shop. This was done and the remaining aircraft backed up the blob and made a splendid, concentrated red ring of fire at which the Lancaster bombing force would aim the loads. The works was destroyed.

'It will be realised that a limitation of marking in this way is that a well-aimed stick of bombs from an early Lancaster might easily scatter the red fire blob, or at least obscure it by smoke. One method of overcoming this problem was by the use of delayed action fuses and detonators in the bombs, only one bomb in each stick being fused to burst on impact in order to give the Controller ("Master Bomber") an indication of the way in which the attack was proceeding. Many highly effective attacks were made against small targets using this refinement.

'Much has been written about the Bomber Command attack on the German tank depot at Mailly Le Camp, near Epernay, on the night of 3/4 May 1944. The operation was executed by 346 Lancasters and Halifaxes of Nos 1 and 5 Groups, led by four Mosquitos of No 617 Squadron supported by eight Mosquitos of No 627 Squadron. The idea was that while the markers of No 617 looked for and marked the target, the No 627 Mossies would dive-bomb anti-aircraft guns in the target area. It was thought that the presence of "dive-bombers" would at least keep the gunners' heads down, and that there might even be the bonus of a few gunners' heads blown off. The target was marked accurately but a delay in relaying information from the Master Bomber to the Main Force occurred. This resulted in the heavies being ordered to orbit north of the target for several minutes in conditions of bright moonlight; a factor which was promptly exploited by the German night fighters. Forty-two of the heavies were lost, and the raid has been described as a disaster *and* a success. If the criterion used to determine success or failure is aircraft and crews lost then by no stretch of the imagination can a loss rate of $12\frac{1}{2}\%$ be termed a success. If, however, an attempt is made to balance the bomber losses against the German loss of an important depot — it was 80% destroyed — together with heavy casualties among trained personnel, particularly senior NCOs, and tanks and other vehicles — and all this with the invasion of Europe only weeks away — then the position becomes very different. Who can say what might have happened if the panzers of Mailly had been able to reach the landing beaches on 5/6 June? That they did not can only be described as a triumph for the Allies.

'To narrow the canvas and relate what happened to just one Mosquito during this important attack will at least give some idea of what could take place on a 5 Group operation. Leonard Cheshire led the four Mosquito markers, and "Bill" Hickox and I were in AZ-G "George" (DZ484) of No 627 Squadron, one of the eight supporting "dive-bombers". So far as we were concerned the approach to the target was uneventful. Just before midnight the Flare Force laid yellow TIs 15 miles north of Mailly, and all the Mosquitos headed for these and set course from them to the target. At 0001 hours, when all good troops should be in barracks, the Flare Force dropped the customary cloud of hooded flares over Mailly, and Cheshire and his men began to search for the depot. At the same time the "dive-bombers" found gun targets and dived on them from 1,500 feet to 500 feet releasing one 500lb bomb per dive. As the eight Mossies each carried four bombs, it will be appreciated that the gunners were at least distracted for a while.

'Meanwhile, at 5,000 feet, the heavies were fighting a deadly battle with German night fighters north of — and later, over — the target. The unfolding engagement could be seen clearly from G-George, in our worm's-eye view position, for at relatively short intervals flames would be seen above and a heavy bomber would begin its death plunge. Sometimes the burning heavy would dive straight towards us and we became exceedingly watchful in case it should crash nearby — with disastrous consequences to ourselves. Our dive-bombing of the guns was

138

therefore interspersed with short dashes away from the trajectory of burning heavies. The raid eventually got into gear and bombs began to crash down on the tank depot. When the "dive-bombers" had finished their task they were ordered to return to base, and by about 0020 hours G-George was on the way home. Since it was manifestly unwise to climb in the target area I stayed at low level and we set course for the French coast. We settled down at about 1,000 feet with a cruising speed of 250mph and for a time all went well.

'The first hint of trouble came when a searchlight shone directly into our cockpit and at the same time a murderous barrage of light flak opened up from below. More lights came on and we were coned. I turned "George" hard to port and dived to about 300 feet above the earth, with "Bill" Hickox exhorting me to "watch the instruments". We were in the unenviable position of a fly jinking close to a moving flypaper in the dark, with an irate householder swatting vigorously as it at the same time — a situation where there is no margin for error. We were literally just above the trees, with the searchlight operators shinging their lights along the ground at us from all sides, while the flak gunners hosed their wares at us along the beams. Not for the first time, "Bill" and I saw streams of flak — red, blue, white and all very pretty — coming towards us; slowly at first but ever-increasing in speed until the individual missiles hurtled overhead and disappeared, to be exploded by their proximity fuses. Sometimes there was a pop or a bang, but G-George kept going.

'This game of cat and mouse continued for many minutes — it seemed like a lifetime. I would turn hard in one direction by about 30 degrees, level out on the new heading for a

Above: Only 32 airmen were awarded a Victoria Cross during 1939-46, and 20 of those were posthumous awards. Leonard Cheshire — seen here being congratulated on his own VC by Flt Lt Keith Astbury DFC — was the only airman of World War 2 to receive this supreme honour for an extended and consistent period of extreme courage and devotion to duty, rather than a single superlative act.

Above right: The view from above Pauillac and Bec d'Ambes, in the Girond Estuary, north of Bordeaux in the evening of 4 August 1944. The targets were oil-storage tanks.

Right: Railway marshalling yards and other communications centres were priority targets throughout 1944-45. The devastation here was at Vaires, Paris.

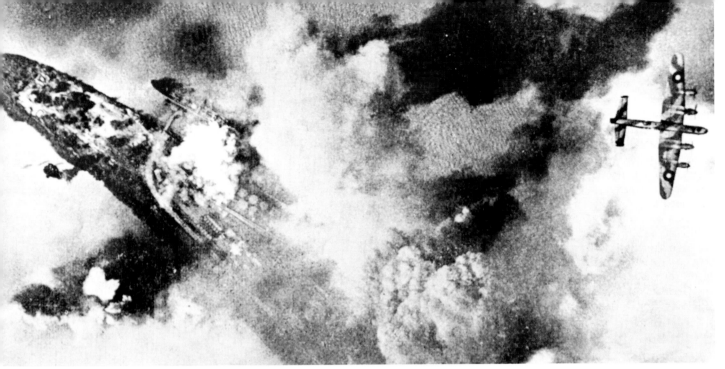

few seconds, then turn hard in the opposite direction by the same amount and fly level on that heading for a brief time. Lest anyone should observe that this was a more-or-less set pattern and a recipe for disaster, I would remind him that we were *very* close to the ground and covering it at high speed; therefore a fleeting target for any particular gunner or searchlight operator. The Germans' best chance of getting us lay in shining the maximum number of searchlights on us in the hope that a mistake would be made and control of the aircraft lost; this they did with great gusto. By the greatest good fortune we were not hit, but I do not recall ever being held in searchlights and under fire for so long and at such low level.

'The end of our ordeal came suddenly when we skipped over the summit of a low hill and there ahead of us lay the sea. I hugged the ground below the crest and "Bill" Hickox and I were treated to a spectacle which we remember vividly to this day. The searchlights were shinging through the trees and above our heads. With the coastline ahead and the lights paradoxically providing some degree of assistance, we now roared along an inlet and past a lighthouse, thence to the open sea and home. The lighthouse proved to be on the coast of Le Treport. I've since visited it, on the ground. It is quite small, and as we were below the level of the light on 4 May 1944, we must have given the occupants of this some-time aid to navigation a very nasty turn indeed — tit for tat . . .

'A regular feature of the "new look" operations was that "wash-ups" were held at Coningsby to assess the methods used and results achieved. These prayer-meetings were useful because they brought the markers and the Flare Force together. At times the meetings became a bit terse when something had gone wrong, and at other times they were hilarious — as when my good friend Flg Off "Googie" Platts was accused by the Base Commander (Air Cdre "Bobby" Sharpe) of marking the right aiming point in the wrong marshalling yard! George Platts could not be termed lucky. After this wrong marshalling yard incident, his run of bad luck continued, as when he took part in an operation against the Phillips Works at Eindhoven, Holland. Searching for the target, flying in and out of cloud, a searchlight suddenly shone directly into his face. Startled, he pulled back on the control column and the Mosquito immediately roared up and over on to its back. "Googie" now found the searchlight apparently above his head so, in his own words, "I half-rolled out and came home". He was not so lucky on 29 June when taking part in a daylight marking sortie against a V-1 weapons' site at Beauvoir. Having completed the marking of the target he set course for home in stepped-down formation with another Mosquito behind and below him. After a short distance a V-1 "doodle bug" was launched from a ramp behind them, and accelerated towards London, only to have its motor fail when below the Mosquitos. It crashed and exploded right underneath them. The lower Mossie was destroyed, while Platt's experienced complete engines' failure. Despite all his efforts the twin Merlins remained silent and he was obliged to land with wheels up and no power. Hitting the ground hard, he broke a leg in the crash landing. However, his navigator was unhurt and, after a brief council of war, they agreed that the nav should make a run for it. This he did but in his haste to get home he fell down a well! There he stayed while a typically thorough Teutonic search failed to find him. At night he identified himself to a French farmer and they devised a scheme whereby the navigator would stay down the well by day and come up for sustenance by night. He was back on the squadron within a few weeks. "Googie" Platts was not so fortunate; he was taken to Germany and spent the rest of the war in Stalag Luft 3.

'Following the notorious Mailly Le Camp attack, 5 Group concentrated its efforts against targets such as railway yards, the bridges over the rivers Loire and Seine, and along the Channel coast. Finally — in the last days before D-Day (6 June) — against the heavy anti-invasion guns along the coastline. Most of these were copybook attacks, with the marker bombs going down on time, and with the heavy supporting bombers dropping their loads in exactly the right place. The experienced marker pilots of No 627 Squadron were by then able to dart in beneath the flares dropped for them by Nos 83 and 97 Squadrons, then to circle and find the aiming point within a couple of minutes and, most important of all, to make accurate shallow dives and drop their spot fires within a very few yards of that point. It's doubtful if any marker pilot could say exactly how he did it; marking a target was largely a matter of practice. In other words the experienced pilot "automatically" positioned his Mosquito in the precise spot from which to make his dive on to the target, dived at the correct angle by placing the aiming point in the right position on his windscreen, released the spot fire by means of a push-button on his control column, and kept the Mosquito in the dive for another two or three seconds to ensure the bombs fell in the desired trajectory. It is on record that marking errors by Mosquitos prior to D-Day were as low as 50 yards, while none — even on the most heavily defended targets, including Brunswick, Munich and Schweinfurt — was greater than 300 yards.

'On a purely personal note, I happened to be a marker for the 5 Group attack on Brunswick on 22 May 1944. On this occasion the AOC decided to employ the principle of offset marking; the idea being to place markers upwind of the target in such a position that they could be seen clearly by Main Force crews throughout the attack and yet could not be blown up by the bombing. The aiming point selected was a park north of the town, and when we arrived — under the usual carpet of flares — we had no difficulty in identifying the park and stoking up a good bonfire in it for the heavies. Moreover, praises be, there was no flak interference. We then sculled around the park, awaiting instructions to either build up the fire of go home. We were eventually told to return to base, and from our viewpoint the raid had been a gift. Not so for the heavies, however, who had difficulty in passing radio messages. The drill was that a proportion of the Flare Force would find the wind on the last leg to the target and pass results to the Flare Force leader. He in turn would calculate the mean wind, pass this to the Master Bomber, who would then work out the wind to be set on bombsights of the Main Force in order to ensure that bombs aimed at the marker flares — our park bonfire — would *undershoot* and hit the target. The trip was not an outstanding success due to the difficulty in getting this false wind broadcast to the Main Force; a communications problem which arose because the W/T system then in use was not sufficiently good. This problem was later overcome by the introduction of VHF radio in heavies — we in Mosquitos had had this aid all the time, and splendid it was. Thereafter 5 Group attacks improved in accuracy, with the important spin-off that morale on the heavy squadrons improved too.

This offset marking technique became a standard 5 Group practice and proved to be enormously effective.

'All depended, however, on accurate placing of a small number of red spot fires, which in turn depended on Mosquito pilots being able to see their target. To illustrate this point, on 28 May our target was the heavy German gun at St Martin de Varreville, just behind what was to be one of the American landing beaches — Utah — on 6 June. These heavy guns were almost invariably defended by light flak, and a barrage of the latter would, of course, betray the gun position. However, on the night in question the German commander held his light AA in check, causing us problems with the target-marking. Although it was a clear night, and the Flare Force had done their job impeccably, we found on crossing the coast that the terrain was uniform, the road running parallel to the sea, while inland there was the usual patchwork of fields with occasional tree-clumps. The gun itself was well camouflaged and we could not find it. We had begun searching at Zero-minus five minutes, but at Zero hour we still hadn't found it. The Main Force arrived but was instructed to orbit — was this to be another Mailly Le Camp? Finally, one of the marker pilots noticed a large "empty" space with tracks leading to it, and reasoned that space like that could not be as blank as it appeared. So the target was marked and the gun destroyed by 100 Lancasters, each carrying armour-piercing bombs. No aircraft was lost on this operation, though I might add that as I laid my spot fires on top of the gun a light-fingered gentleman in a Lancaster above decided to drop his load. The stick fell short but "Bill" Hickox and I heard the crump-crump of bombs coming up behind us — we were not amused! This attack merely emphasised just how the best-laid schemes of men "oft gang agley" . . .

'After the D-Day landings had taken place, and No 627's hectic spell in the Transportation Plan was over, it was time to send some of the senior crews on rest. Thus our popular CO — Wing Commander Roy Elliott — and one of the Flight commanders, "Rocky" Nelles, both of whom had been with the squadron since its formation, were posted. In July a number of other crews found themselves on the way to other units — including "Bill" Hickox and me. "Bill" and I went back to 8 Group, to the training unit at Warboys, near Huntingdon. He went to the Navigation Section, while I was sent to the Mosquito Dual Flight. I stayed with this unit — 1655 Mosquito TU, later 16 OTU — from July 1944 until April 1947, as pilot instructor, Flight commander, and eventually Chief Instructor.

Above: **Mosquitos of B Flight, 16 OTU, Cottesmore. GA-F at right was RR292.**

'I feel I ought to add a little about No 627 and the two Lancaster Path Finder squadrons Nos 83 and 97. All had been "attached" to 5 Group from 8 Group in April 1944, and stayed with 5 Group until the war ended. Naturally, everyone had a fierce loyalty to 8 Group at the time of the move, and there was a certain amount of resentment at being shipped off to another Group. Nevertheless, it is also true that we quickly saw what a war-winner the low-marking technique was, and we developed a loyalty to 5 Group. Perhaps in reality our loyalties were evenly divided. The AOC would have noticed this and would undoubtedly have preferred crews from within 5 Group, or men who had completed an ops' tour in the Group. Anyway, the new CO and Flight commanders of No 627 were all 5 Group men. The crews continued to be trained at 1655 MTU and, as far as I'm aware, there was never a comeback on this score.

'As far as No 627 was concerned, the squadron continued to operate skilfully against all kinds of targets — marking on behalf of 5 Group and, at times, for No 617 Squadron. The off-set marking technique reached a very high level of efficiency on 11 September 1944, when 218 Lancasters, led by four Mosquito markers, destroyed Darmstadt. The aiming point was a parade ground one mile west of the town centre, and here a bonfire of red spot fires was lit. The clump of red markers was backed up with greens, and the Master Bomber then called in the Main Force who attacked on no less than seven different headings and at varying times of release to give the maximum bombing spread. To summarise what I thought of No 627 Squadron, two words will suffice - "Just great".'

Canal-Busters
MAURICE A. SMITH DFC

Above: Gaggle. Sextet of No 619 Squadron Lancasters heading for Germany, February 1944, from Coningsby. Formed as a Lanc unit on 18 April 1943, the squadron was disbanded on 18 July 1945; one of the relatively few RAF squadrons never to be granted an official badge or motto. *IWM*

'Germany's communications were under almost continuous attack after D-Day. Railways and their marshalling yards had little respite; Baltic ports and shipping were hit; the sea approaches and river mouths were mined — in all of which Bomber Command was very active. These attacks were both tactical and strategic. In the co-ordinated plan of late 1944, which had the specific purpose of ending the war as quickly as possible, zones were defined for attention and, in addition, five specific interdiction targets. Two of these were main-line railway viaducts and three were sections of canal. Then, as now, a chain of great canals formed a most important part of Germany's industrial transport system.

'Some stretches of these huge canals run above the level of the countryside; rivers and even roads pass under them. It was not too difficult a task to pulverise their embankments with loads of high explosive bombs and so empty the canals for several miles, stranding the long barges and incidentally causing local flooding. Two such vulnerable raised stretches selected for attack were on the Dortmund Ems Canal near Ladbergen (between Munster and Rheine), where it briefly divides into two channels, and the Mitteland Canal near Gravenhorst, close to its junction with the Dortmund Ems. These are in the area just to the north of the Ruhr, and the two canals connect this huge industrial area with Hannover, Brunswick, and Berlin to the east.

'For us — navigator Lee Page, me and Mosquito BXX, KB401 "Easy" — the night of 4/5 November 1944, with the Dortmund Ems Canal as our target, started badly. Our morale was always low before take-off, mainly because we operated alone and still missed the bustle and chatter of a squadron departure and the close presence of our Lanc crew of seven. Controllers of 5 Group flew from Coningsby, which was 54 Base HQ and also housed Nos 83 and 97 Squadrons. The Mosquito marker force of No 627 Squadron flew from nearby Woodhall Spa. The Lanc squadrons trundled off an hour or more before our solitary Mossie (we pronounced the "ss" as "Z's") was due to get airborne. We would start up on the silent tarmac, using only a flash lamp to see by, check time and taxi out for our solitary take-off. At least Flying Control would tell the Ops Room we had gone. "Easy" had been over to No 627 Squadron for servicing and had flown back that morning. She started well and the Packard-built Rolls-Royce Merlins ran up OK. This was only a three-hours sortie, so our 100-gallon auxiliary tanks under the wings were only half-full. Our load was one yellow and two red target indicators (TIs) - red for marking, yellow to cancel any stray red or German spoof marking.

'We lined up on the string of tiny runway

Left: Wg Cdr Maurice A. Smith DFC (seated centre) with his first Lancaster crew. *'Autocar'*

lights, opened up against the brakes and started our run. Differential throttle, then rudder to check swing as the tail came up and, at 105 knots, off into the night. Almost immediately the engine notes sounded wrong and the aircraft yawed as we climbed. Check both throttles and bang pitch levers forward on their stops. Wheels up, climbing at 160 knots, height 500 feet, straight ahead. The starboard engine seemed to roar and the aircraft tried to slew to port. Perhaps the port engine had cut? No, all seemed normal there; instruments, noise, exhaust flames long and lilac blue as they should be. Again the roar and lurch, and this time the starboard rev counter sailed up somewhere near the 3,500 mark. We had a prop trying to run away.

'In a few seconds of surprise and diagnosis we reached 800 feet, levelled out and throttled right back on the starboard engine. There was no question of pressing on, so we must land back. I decided not to feather the starboard airscrew. The engine was unlikely to come to more harm and could help in an emergency. A Mossie would not go round again on one engine from ground level with flaps and wheels down, so we would be committed at around 400 feet on the approach (Thought! "When did I last practise a single-engine landing at night?") Now No 627 Squadron would have a stand-by aircraft ready to go at Woodhall Spa — we did not have one at Coningsby. Marker Leader

would be quite capable of controlling the operation if we did not show up — so long as he got there. No, let's have a go. Break radio silence and try to sound like a training flight. Tell Woodhall you want to land and take up a spare aircraft. They will guess what's going on.

'They did. We landed without incident and leaped into a strange Mosquito IV, DZ418 "Baker", looked round its unfamiliar instruments, started up and taxied out. Quick engine check and away up to 10,000 feet on course. We flew at 2,850rpm +9lb/sq in, cut corners on our dog-leg course in dark, cloudless sky, and were near enough to see the first parachute flares fall, some minutes before the attack was due to begin. We had stuffed the nose of the Mosquito down for the last ten minutes, holding about 360 knots and arriving in the Ladbergen area at 1,200 feet. Sqn Ldr Churcher had got things started. Visibility was good. Using their usual dive-bombing techniques the Mossies now put their red TIs on the aiming point.

'The VHF talk would have gone something like this starting at zero hour minus 10 minutes:

"Controller to Marker Leader, how do you hear me? Over." No reply probably out of range. Zero minus nine minutes, call repreated.

"ML to C, clear threes." (Meaning plainly heard but rather distant.)

"C to ML. I am running two minutes late. Can see the flares. Please start the marking."

"ML to C. Roger."

"Marker 4, Tally Ho." (Meaning that No 4 of the six Mosquito low-level markers has found the marking point and is diving in to put a red TI on the spot.)

"ML to Marker Force, that TI is 200 yards NE of the point. Back it up south." (ML has decided to accept an error, when backed up south, of about 100 yards.)

"C to ML. I'm with you."

ML to C. Roger, handing over."

"C to MF. Back up red TI to south."

"Marker 3, Tally Ho" . . . *"Marker 2, Tally Ho."*

"C to MF. Thank you, that is enough. Clear the area."

"C to Codeword Force, come in and aim at group of red TIs as planned. Codeword Force, aim at red TIs as planned."

'A great gaggle of 170 Main Force Lancs dropped their full loads of 14 1,000lb bombs, many with long delay fuses to add to the confusion on the ground. Some early loads fell too far east, but the error was noticed and corrected. The flares had blown away and long gone out, and even the target marking was practically obliterated. The attack was short and concentrated; 930 tons of bombs fell, all but 5% dropped in a circle of 530 yards radius about the MPI. This worked out at about 25 1,000lb bombs per acre, the best concentration achieved by the Group to date. Tomorrow's PRU photos would show the extent of damamge and success. Three aircraft had been lost, two to fighters after leaving the target area; and two enemy fighters were claimed shot down.

'Two nights later, we were briefed for a similar attack on the Mitteland Canal at Gravenhorst, only about 15 miles north of Ladbergen. We still hadn't got our Mosquito "Easy" back, so were using a borrowed Mk IV, DZ 518 "Mike". The weather was to be similar, but with more haze and a stronger wind. The actual marking point was not very clearly defined, and we studied the area and the buildings, memorising any features — railway line, salt pans — that might stand out. This time we flew out more steadily to flight plan, with a little more time in hand.

'As we turned into our last leg for run-in, we saw occasional searchlight beams fanning around to starboard. Quite suddenly a ruddy great violet-white beam opened up bang on to us, followed at once by others. We had heard about so-called master beams, so perhaps this was one of them. But there should not have been so many lights in the gap between Rheine and Munster. We were at an effective height for predicted flak which would probably follow. And it did — but we had moved over, luckily without the search-

144

lights following. The time between guns firing and their shells bursting worked out as a count of one second per thousand feet. (Experts might disagree for the "88s" with their high muzzle velocity.) At 12,000 feet, about 12 seconds from gun flash. If you dived 30 degrees to port and looked high to starboard, there was a good chance of seeing flak burst where you would have been had you kept straight on. We were glad to be in a manoeuvrable Mossie rather than a Lanc or — Lord help us — a Stirling. A solitary aircraft was always more vulnerable, and this was one big worry for single Mosquitos and even more for a Main Force bomber that got winged and became a straggler without even "Window" protection. The first bursts had missed us and we could quickly jink out of range, but why this nasty reception over what should have been open country? Voice from navigator: *"Should be about 12 minutes to go, Skip. I reckon that was Munster. We are a bit off course and ahead of time."* Too right, and our first hint of a Met error on wind strength.

'For a final, accurate positioning beyond Gee range the Mosquito force in particular, with their more limited space and navigational equipment, depended on a few selected Pathfinder Lancs with all the "blind" aids including H2S radar to drop green pro-

Above: The notorious Dortmund-Ems Canal, a constant target for Bomber Command throughout the war. Two VCs ware awarded to bomber crew members involved in attacks on this vital waterway; seen here in late 1944.

ximity indicators as near the aiming point as possible. Similar guidance was sometimes given for track turning points. We waited hopefully as we dived gently in the approximate direction of the target and identified with the Marker Leader. No greens. No parachute flares yet.

'There was an amber-tinged haze in a dark sky and nothing could be seen below. At long last a few flares showed ahead and left of us, and beyond, a glimpse of a green TI. A quick caustic word to the navigator and dive hard over towards them. Faint reflections showed here and thereon the ground which could have been water or glass. As we dived lower we saw even less. A few flares backed up the dying light of the first ones. Anxious call to Marker Leader. Only about four minutes to go. He was searching. A few more scattered flares were dropping, but at 800 feet there was not a single recognisable feature below. The German blackout was faultless. I had a frightful mental picture of the Main Force bearing down like a great herd of elephants and even more difficult to stop. Search harder. Tip the Mossie on edge. Marker 4 says he has found the salt pans but practically no flares there to help. Call Flare Force Lancs and Backers-Up for anything they've got left — knowing most, if not all, have already flown over.

"Marker 3. Tally Ho!" Thank God for that Marker. Where is he? Marker 2 calls for more flares. Just time to save the operation. Call up Main Force to delay their arrival by two minutes — dog-leg or orbit. I could just imagine what those crews were calling us. Marker 2 is not able to back up. No longer sees the solitary TI. Marker 3 was sure he had found the spot, but the TI must have gone into the canal and been extinguished. No flares left. Four minutes after H-hour. Despairing effort; full throttle climb to 2,000 feet for a more vertical view and maybe a glimpse of a silver thread of canal. No hope. Too late. Attack should have been over by now. Dangerous to keep the Main Force milling around any more — half Germany must know we are blundering around the sky north of the Rhur. "Abortive code sign to Codeword Force. Go home. Go home." There was no alternative target. In fact 30 of the Lancs, including markers, got their loads away, presumably blind, using their own H2S. Most of the bombs had delay fuses, so we did not see them explode. Marker and Flare Force Lancs usually filled up any spare (bomb) stations in their bomb bays with thousand-pounders.

'A frightful nightmarish experience it was. What on earth could one say to the AOC — who expected a direct, personal call and first assessment, day or night, as soon as the Controller landed back and found a scrambler 'phone in the de-briefing room? A raid assessment showed that an exceptional combination of troubles had made this attack abortive. A much stronger wind than expected blew such parachute flares as there were away to the east and scattered them. No fewer than seven of the 14 Flare Force, plus four Blind Marker Lancaster crews, had suffered H2S radar failures. The one target indicator that Mosquito Marker 3 got down in about the right place fell into the water and could not be seen or backed up by the others. The green proximity markers — two in this case — which were sometimes accurate enough to serve as emergency aiming points, could not be assessed and were confused with a green route marker. Anything other than accurate bombing on such a target, out in open country, would have been useless.

'Unhappily, 10 of the 235 aircraft were lost, for reasons not altogether clear. The relatively bright sky and good upper visibility helped enemy fighters in the target area and on the way back. The confusion and concentration of aircraft around the target would have been conducive to collisions. Landing back with a full bomb load was no one's idea of a picnic . . .

'Of course, the Group went back to the Mitteland Canal a couple of weeks later, and with only slight opposition found and emptied it properly. Then, a month later, when frantic work on the part of the Germans had just finished patching it up for use again, it took an even bigger pounding, this time in daylight. At the same time the Dortmund Ems was also successfully attacked and emptied. Traffic through Munster Locks was reduced from a 1944 montly average of 844,000 tons to north and east, and 585,000 tons from north and east, to 14,000 tons and 11,000 tons respectively in January 1945. Extracts from official reports speak of 5 Group's second attack on Ladbergen; it "breached the canal at the same place, but this time the breach on the western by-pass was much wider. The eastern by-pass was also hit and two lengths of the embankment totalling about 1,500 feet were destroyed. Two bombs pierced the viaduct over the river Glane . . . the water, carrying barges with it, flowing into the surrounding countryside. The Mitteland Canal was also drained for the first 18 miles because a safety gate was left open."

'To quote from the *Strategic Air Offensive against Germany 1939-45, Vol 3,* on the programme of canal-bursting raids: "It may be doubted whether the accuracy, regularity and effectiveness of those brilliant operations had ever, in combination, been approached by any air force in the previous history of bombing." '

Below: **Sqn Ldr R. G. Churcher DFC in a Lancaster of No 619 Squadron, February 1944.** *IWM*

Home is the Hunter

At the cessation of hostilities in Europe, RAF Bomber Command was immediately tasked with several purely peaceful roles. Of these perhaps the most satisfying, from the air crews' viewpoint, were the 'operations' concerned with repatriating Allied prisoners of war from various 'collecting points' in France, Germany and Italy et al. Flt Lt D. C. Tritton, having completed one operational tour with No 49 Squadron in 1944, returned to the ops' scene in March 1945, joining No 189 Squadron at Fulbeck, an airfield shared at that time with this old unit. Though briefed for sorties on many occasions thereafter, in fact he only took part in one operation prior to VE-Day; such was the uncertainty of the operational scene in those final weeks of war. In his own words:

'In April 1945 my squadron (No 189) moved to Bardney, sharing the accommodation there with No 9 Squadron, and from here I was involved in two different types of operations ferrying personnel. The first was on VE-Day (8 May) which is remembered as a Spartan day for the inner man. After lunchtime six Lancasters of No 189 Squadron left Bardney — No 9 Squadron had been stood down — for Juvincourt, near Rheims. A sandwich lunch had been provided. The scene at Juvincourt under a hot sun was both impressive and moving. Our brief was to ferry 24 newly-released prisoners of war to Westcott, Buckinghamshire, a reception centre for returning ex-prisoners.

'On arrival at Juvincourt the Lancasters (from many squadrons throughout the command) were marshalled in echelon for the length of one side of a spare runway; a most impressive sight and certainly the greatest number I ever saw on the ground together. Simultaneous with the arrival of the Lancasters was the movement of large US

articulated lorries with high slatted sides, each containing our passengers-to-be. These moved up along the opposite side of the runway, each stopping opposite a Lancaster. As each bomber taxied into position and cut engines, wild cheering broke out from the ex-prisoners standing in the lorries. When the Lancaster arrivals ceased the lorries were emptied and parties of 24 men came across the runway to be lifted out. They were lean and bronzed and appeared to be healthy and vigorous. All were dressed in khaki with no insignia, though some declared themselves to be bomber crew.

'We arrived at Westcott at 2020 and the ex-prisoners were whisked away. The local WVS supplied crews with a cup of tea and a rock cake, taken standing alfresco, and then away to Bardney. A solitary airman chocked the Lancasters after our landing at 2125. No transport had been sent, so we walked the mile or so to the billet to wash and change, then another mile or so back to the hangar where the gigantic all-ranks "Victory Party" was taking place. Failing to find any food on the cleared tables, I approached the Group Captain and enquired of our food. He looked horrified and then confessed that we had been forgotten, but suggested that we console ourselves with a free drink. Alas! Too late! The last pints were being served as we reached the bar . . .

'The other passenger-ferrying operation was Operation "Dodge", which required us

Above: Mercy mission. Loading a Lanc with bulk food bags for dropping over Holland, May 1945. A Lancaster load of such provisions was estimated to be capable of feeding 3,280 people for a day.

Right: Exodus. A scene on Frankfurt airfield on 7 May 1945, with Wg Cdr Ian Hay (right) and his navigator Flg Off 'Art' Boys (left) supplying a fellow Aussie ex-prisoner of war with rations. Hay was OC No 467 Squadron RAAF and skipper of Lancaster R5868, 'S' (behind) which was the first Lancaster to land in Germany for 'Exodus' evacuation flights.

to ferry relief troops to Pomigliano, near Naples, and bring back men in the LIAP ("Leave in Anticipation of Python") scheme; "Python" being the operational code word for service in the Far East. "Dodge" was undertaken late in September 1945 and troops involved were thus due for peace-keeping duties, not front line war service. The long haul was relieved a little for the soldiers, compared with the repatriation of ex-prisoners, for only 20 passengers were lifted in each Lancaster. Blankets were provided as we needed to fly at a higher altitude en route. A brigadier we carried was fortunately wearing battledress and we put him in the nose. It turned out to be an Irish compliment because the front turret developed an hydraulic oil leak, and the poor chap just didn't seem to be safe from it wherever he moved!

'Our first attempt to return nearly resulted in the loss of the aircraft and all on board. Relatively high cumulus cloud forced us to climb higher than we wished, with the soldiers not equipped with oxygen. After three attempts and failing to break out of the rough cloud, we tried sneaking underneath 800 feet. Soon after the low cloud roof extended over us we were caught by a vertical current which instantly turned us on to our side. We plunged straight down and I shudder to think how close we were to the sea when we recovered. The soldiers were cut, bruised and battered and also suffered

torn clothing. Having only gone a few miles beyond Rome we decided to take the soldiers back to allow them to sort themselves out. On arrival several swore that they would never fly again, and much discussion took place about going home overland.

'A few days later we arrived at our aircraft to come home with what we assumed was a fresh batch of soldiers. Looking at one man I said, "I've seen you before. Were you with us on Friday?". "Yes, sir," came the reply, "We all asked to go home with the same crew!" Just after the Italian trip, I cut off the Group Captain's tie at a Mess party, and within a week a new phase of RAF life had begun for me — with seaplanes, in Scotland. Whether the latter two events were connected has always been an interesting speculation . . . '

Above: Peace. The return to peace also meant a return to more 'airmanlike' appearances, as on this AOC's Inspection at Bardney in 1945. The AOC, AVM Constantine, is followed by Grp Capt Howard (Station commander), the Base Commander, and Grp Capt Bearn (SASO), plus the usual trailing entourage of lesser minions deemed necessary on such occasions. *D. C. Tritton*

Left: Operation 'Dodge' — evacuation and repatriation of army personnel from Italy etc. This mass of Lancasters engaged in 'Dodge' were from Nos 15, 44, 138 and 150 squadrons, on Pomagliano airfield. Nearest aircraft, KM-N was PD332 of No 44. *J. Chatterton DFC*

Gallery

Left: Wg Cdr Roderick Alistair Brook Learoyd VC, the first Bomber Command VC of the war, awarded for his attack on the Dortmund-Ems Canal in a No 49 Squadron Hampden on 12/13 August 1940.
British Official

Below left: Flt Lt (Acting Sqn Ldr) James Anderson Pitcairn-Hill, DSO, DFC of No 83 Squadron. Born in Fife, he joined the RAF as a Halton Apprentice, gained a cadetship to Cranwell (along with Peter Wykeham Barnes), and eventually joined No 83 Squadron at Scampton. Flying Hampdens, he was awarded both the DSO and DFC in 1940 but was killed by flak in Hampden P1183 on 18/19 September 1940 over the French coast.
Mrs Harrison

Below: Flt Sgt John Hannah, a Wireless Operator/AG of No 83 Squadron who, at 18 years of age, became the youngest-ever air VC for extinguishing a mid-air fire in his Hampden on 15/16 September 1940. Invalided from the RAF in December 1942, he died of tuberculosis on 7 June 1947.

Above left: **Flg Off Leslie Thomas Manser** of No 50 Squadron who was awarded a posthumous VC for selfless courage in attempting to save the lives of his crippled Avro Manchester's crew during the first '1,000-bomber' raid on Cologne on 30/31 May 1942. *C. Manser*

Above: **'Gibbo' — Wg Cdr Guy Penrose Gibson VC, DSO, DFC** who flew a total of 177 operational sorties (76 as a bomber pilot, the rest as a night fighter), but whose name will always be associated with the No 617 Squadron attack on German dams on 16/17 May 1943. He died flying a Mosquito as Master Bomber for a raid at Rheydt and Müchen Gladbach on the night of 19 September 1944. *IWM*

Left: **Sqn Ldr Hugh Everitt DSO, DFC** who completed two tours of operations, the second with No 50 Squadron.

Above right: **Dam-busters.** Five Australian members of the original No 617 Squadron. From left: J. F. Leggo DFC, T. D. Simpson DFM, R. C. Hay DFC, B. T. Foxlee DFM, and H. B. 'Micky' Martin DSO, DFC. *IWM*

Right: **Flt Lt William 'Bill' Reid VC** received his award for completing a bombing sortie against Dusseldorf on 3/4 November 1943, despite wounds and severe damage to his No 61 Squadron Lancaster. Seen here with that crew's survivors: (back) L. S. Rolton; A. F. Emerson; and (front) J. W. Norris and G. C. Baldwin. He later served with No 617 Squadron but was shot down on 31 July 1944 and became a PoW. *W. Reid VC*

Above left: **Grp Capt Leonard Cain Slee DSO, DFC who served at one period with No 49 Squadron.** *IWM*

Above: **Wg Cdr W. A. 'Bill' Forbes DSO, DFC, RAAF who came from Queensland, Australia, and commanded No 463 Squadron from late 1944. He was killed in action on 21 February 1945.** *S. Bridgeman*

Left: **Wg Cdr David M. Balme DSO, DFC of No 227 Squadron.** *IWM*

Right: **Flg Off (later Sqn Ldr) T. N. Scholefield RAAF, from Cryon, New South Wales, Australia who flew with No 467 Squadron RAAF.** *Central Press*

Right: Sqn Ldr (later Grp Capt) John Searby, DSO, DFC, who served in No 106 Squadron, then, when with No 83 Squadron inaugurated the role of 'Master of Ceremonies' (Master Bomber) for the famous attack on Peenemunde on 17/18 August 1943. An ex-Halton Apprentice, he eventually retired as Air Cdre CBE, DSO, DFC. *IWM*

Far right, top: Flt Sgt G. E. A. Pendrill, DFM of No 97 Squadron, killed in action. *IWM*

Below right: The immortal erk. An unidentified ground crew man of No 619 Squadron, February 1944; representing the multitude of unpublicised 'erks' without whose labours and dedication the bomber war could not have triumphed. . . *IWM*

Far right, bottom: Lt (later maj) Hubert C. Knilans DSO, DFC, American DFC USAAF — 'Nick' — who flew 51 sorties with the RAF, including No 617 Squadron, piling up 305 operational hours over Germany. He now resides in Canada. *H. C. Knilans*

Above: Sqn Ldr Jack Vivian DSO, DFC of No 57 Squadron. *IWM*

Above right: Flt Sgt George Thompson, from Perthshire, a wireless operator on No 9 Squadron, who on New Year's Day, 1945, during a raid on the Dortmund–Ems Canal, sacrificed his own life attempting to save the lives of his burning Lancaster's two air gunners. He was awarded a posthumous VC.

Right: Grp Capt Leonard Cheshire VC, DSO, DFC and WO Norman C. Jackson VC. The latter, a flight engineer with No 106 Squadron, received his award for climbing out on the wing of his crippled Lancaster over Schweinfurt, attempting to extinguish an engine fire on 26 April 1944.

In Tribute

Below: **Lancaster PA474, dips its wings in salute over Lincoln Cathedral — an edifice probably best-known of all to the thousands of 5 Group air crews throughout the war.**

Appendices

1 Air Officers Commanding-in-Chief, 5 Group

Air Cdre	W. B. Callaway AFC	17 August 1937
AVM	A. T. Harris OBE, AFC	11 September 1939
AVM	N. R. Bottomley CIE, DSO, AFC	22 November 1940
AVM	J. C. Slessor DSO, MC	12 May 1941
AVM	W. A. Coryton MVO, DFC	25 April 1942
AVM	Hon R. A. Cochrane CBE, AFC	28 February 1943
AVM	H. A. Constantine CBE, DSO	16 January 1945

5 Group disbanded on 15 December 1945

2 Orders of Battle

26 September 1939 Total: 128 aircraft

Squadron	Base Airfield	Aircraft	Remarks
44	Waddington	Hampden	
49	Scampton	Hampden	
50	Waddington	Hampden	
61	Hemswell	Hampden	
83	Scampton	Hampden	
106	Cottesmore	Hampden	Reserve sqn
144	Hemswell	Hampden	
185	Cottesmore	Hampden	Reserve sqn

25 January 1942 Total: 268 aircraft (14 Lancasters, 62 Manchesters, 192 Hampdens)

44	Waddington	Lancaster	Non-operational
49	Scampton	Hampden	
50	Swinderby	Hampden	
61	North Luffenham	Manchester	
83	Scampton	Hampden/Manchester	
97	Coningsby	Manchester	
106	Coningsby	Hampden	
144	North Luffenham	Hampden	
207	Bottesford	Manchester	
408 RCAF	Syerston	Hampden	
420 RCAF	Waddington	Hampden	
455 RAAF	Swinderby	Hampden	

4 February 1943 Total: 335 aircraft (183 Lancasters, 152 various)

9	Waddington	Lancaster
44	Waddington	Lancaster
49	Fiskerton	Lancaster
50	Skellingthorpe	Lancaster
57	Scampton	Lancaster
61	Syerston	Lancaster
97	Woodhall Spa	Lancaster
106	Syerston	Lancaster

Squadron	Base Airfield	Aircraft	Remarks
207	Langar	Lancaster	
467 RAAF	Bottesford	Lancaster	
1506 BAT Flt	Waddington	Oxford	
1514 BAT Flt	Coningsby	Oxford	
1518 BAT Flt	Dunholme Lodge	Oxford	
1485 BGF	Fulbeck	Various	
ABTF	Fulbeck	Oxford	
1654 CU	Wigsley	Lancaster/Manchester/ Halifax	
1660 CU	Swinderby	Lancaster/Manchester	
1661 CU	Winthorpe	Lancaster/Manchester	

22 March 1945 Total: 371 aircraft (341 Lancasters, 30 Mosquitos)

9	Bardney	Lancaster	
44	Spilsby	Lancaster	
49	Fulbeck	Lancaster	
50	Skellingthorpe	Lancaster	
57	East Kirkby	Lancaster	
61	Skellingthorpe	Lancaster	
83	Coningsby	Lancaster	'On loan' from PFF
97	Coningsby	Lancaster	'On loan' from PFF
106	Metheringham	Lancaster	
189	Fulbeck	Lancaster	
207	Spilsby	Lancaster	
227	Balderton	Lancaster	
463 RAAF	Waddington	Lancaster	
467 RAAF	Waddington	Lancaster	
617	Woodhall Spa	Lancaster/Mosquito	
619	Strubby	Lancaster	
627	Woodhall Spa	Mosquito/Lancaster	'On loan' from PFF
630	East Kirkby	Lancaster	
1690 BDT Flt	Metheringham		
1695 BDT Flt	Dishforth		

3   5 Group Operational Airfields, 1939-45

Airfield	Squadrons resident at some period
Bardney	9, 189, 227
Bottesford	207, 467 RAAF
Coningsby	9, 57, 61, 83, 97, 106, 617, 619
Cottesmore	44, 57, 106, 195, 207
East Kirkby	57, 630
Finningley	106
Fiskerton	49
Fulbeck	49, 189
Grantham	106, 113, 211
Hemswell	57, 61, 83, 97, 144
Langar	207
Metheringham	106, 189, 467 RAAF
Mildenhall	44, 207, 211
Newton	Satellite field
North Luffenham	61, 144, 408 RCAF
Scampton	9, 49, 57, 83, 467 RAAF, 617
Skellingthorpe	50, 61, 463 RAAF, 619
Spilsby	44, 207
Strubby	227, 619
Swinderby	50, 455 RAAF
Syerston	49, 61, 106, 408 RCAF
Tollerton	Satellite field
Waddington	9, 44, 49, 50, 57, 61, 83, 97, 207, 420 RCAF, 463 RAAF, 467 RAAF, 617
Woodhall Spa	97, 617, 619, 627

Bibliography

Barker, R.; *The 1000 Plan*; Chatto & Windus, 1965. *Strike Hard, Strike Sure*; Chatto & Windus, 1963.

Bekker, C.; *The Luftwaffe War Diaries*; Macdonald, 1967.

Bowyer, C.; *Guns in the Sky — The Air Gunners*; J. M. Dent, 1979. *For Valour — The Air VCs*; Kimber, 1978. *Hampden Special*; Ian Allan, 1976. *Mosquito at War*; Ian Allan, 1973.

Bowyer, M. J. F. & Sharp, M.; *Mosquito*; Faber, 1967.

Boyle, A.; *No Passing Glory*; J. Collins, 1955.

Braddon, R.; *Cheshire, VC*; Evans Bros, 1954.

Brickhill, P.; *The Dambusters*; Evans Bros, 1951.

Bushby, J.; *Gunner's Moon*; Ian Allan, 1972.

Caidin, M.; *The Night Hamburg Died*; Ballantine, 1960.

Cheshire, L., VC; *Bomber Pilot*; Hutchinson, 1943. *The Face of Victory*; Hutchinson, 1961.

Crown Copyright; *Log Book of Wg Cdr G. P. Gibson, VC;* 1976.

Currie J.; *Lancaster Target*; New English Library, 1977.

Finn, S.; *Lincolnshire Air War 1939-45*; Aero Litho Co, 1973.

Galland, A.; *The First & the Last*; Methuen, 1955.

Gibson, G. P., VC; *Enemy Coast Ahead*; M. Joseph, 1946.

Goulding, B. & Garbett, M.; *Lancaster at War*; Ian Allan, 1971.

Hancock, T. N.; *Bomber County (Lincolnshire)*; Lincs Library, 1978.

Harris, A. T.; *Bomber Offensive*; Collins, 1947.

Herington, J.; *RAAF Official History*; 2 Vols, AWM, 1963.

Heilmann, W.; *Alert in the West*; Kimber, 1955.

Irving, D.; *The Destruction of Dresden*; Kimber, 1963.

Jefford, C. G.; *History of RAF Scampton*; Delta Magazine, 1968.

Johnson F. (Ed); *RAAF over Europe*; Eyre & Spottiswoode, 1946.

Kennedy, L.; *Menace — The Tirpitz*; BCA, London, 1979.

Kostenuk & Griffin; *RCAF Squadrons*; CWM, 1977.

Lawrence, W. J.; *No 5 Bomber Group*; Faber & Faber, 1951.

Mason, T.; *9 Squadron*; Beaumont Aviation, 1965. *12 Squadron — Leads the Field*; Private, 1960.

Middlebrook, M.; *The Nuremburg Raid*; Allen Lane, 1973.

Moyes, P. J. R.; *Bomber Squadrons of the RAF*; Macdonald, 1964.

OUP; *RCAF Overseas etc*; 3 Vols, 1944-49.

Price, A. W.; *Instruments of Darkness*; Kimber, 1967. *Battle over the Reich*; Ian Allan, 1973.

Richards & Saunders; *Royal Air Force, 1939-45*; 3 Vols, HMSO, 1953-54.

Roberts, N.; *Lancaster Crash Log*; Private, 1974.

Robertson, B.; *Lancaster*; Harleyford, 1964.

Saward, D.; *The Bombers' Eye*; Cassell, 1959.

Searby, J.; *The Great Raids — Peenemunde*; Nutshell Press, 1978. *The Great Raids — Essen*; Nutshell Press, 1979.

Thompson, H. L.; *RNZAF Official History*; 3 Vols, RNZAF, 1953-59.

Walker, N.; *Strike to Defend*; Spearman, 1963.

Webster & Frankland; *Strategic Air Offensive*; 4 Vols, HMSO, 1961.

White, A.; *44 Squadron History*; Private, 1978.

No 5 Group Roll of Honour; 1949.